Praise for Taming Tigers

C000056516

"motivational and inspirationa
Ali Faramawy
Area Vice President, Microsoft Middle East & Africa, Vice President, Microsoft International

"Not only are the theories relevant and logical but proven by Jim's life experience"
Steve Woolridge
Area Director, Lloyds TSB Commercial

"Inspirational, highly motivating and informative"
Dr Terry Tucker
Director of Learning, Development & Hospitality, Barchester Healthcare

"an inspiration and great fun"
Neil Mullarkey
Co-Founder The Comedy Store Players and L. Vaughan Spencer's alter-ego

"Everyone should hear Jim's story and 'Taming Tigers' principles"
Jack Bush
Director, Global Pharmaceutical Marketing Intelligence, ALCON Laboratories INC

"truly outstanding and unique"
Joe D Adams
Chairman for Group 11 & Leaders Forum 6, Founder and Managing Director of Adams & Associates (UK) Ltd, The Academy for Chief Executives

"Simply outstanding!"
Dave Muller
CEO, Suffolk New College

"truly inspirational and more importantly 100% effective"
Phil Boyle
General Manager, BT Major Business

TAMING TIGERS

By

JIM LAWLESS

A Taming Tigers Book

First Published in Great Britain in 2008
by Taming Tigers Publishing.

Copyright © 2008 by Jim Lawless

The moral right of the author has been asserted.

Jim Lawless has asserted his right under Copyright Designs and Patents Act 1988 to
be identified as the author of the work.

All rights reserved.

No part of this publication may be reproduced, stored in a retrieval system, or trans-
mitted in any form or by any means without the prior permission in writing of the
publisher, nor be otherwise circulated in any form of binding or cover other than that
in which it is published without a similar condition including this condition being
imposed on the subsequent purchaser.

A CIP Catalogue record for this book is available from the British Library.

ISBN: 978-0-956-0815-0-6

Printed in Great Britain by the MPG Books Group, Bodmin and King's Lynn
Typeset by Hope Services (Abingdon) Ltd
Taming Tigers Publishing — Part of the Taming Tigers Group

www.tamingtigers.com

"The views, thoughts and opinions expressed in the case studies and testimonials repre-
sent the personal views, thoughts and opinions of the named individuals concerned and
are not necessarily endorsed or shared by the named employer of such individuals".

Thanks to At The Races, James House, 18–21 Corsham Street, London, N1 6DR
for allowing permission to reproduce images.

Picture of 222 Gray's Inn Road by R Sones used under the terms of the
"Creative Commons Licence".

Thanks also to Terry Beasley, Ross MacLennan and Liz Amairee for
permission to reproduce the photographs of Jim speaking in London,
in Barcelona and riding in Epsom respectively

To Maddie and Gee

Acknowledgements

Getting Taming Tigers to this stage has been a collaborative affair.

First, thanks must go to all of the audience members and workshop delegates who have given invaluable comment and advice and, often, stayed in contact.

I owe a great debt to Michael Caulfield for starting the racing project off, Tina Fletcher for teaching me to ride, Mark Bradburne for his constant help and advice, Martin and Sarah Bosley (and all the members of "Team Bos") for their endless encouragement and support, Charlie Morlock (and all of the Raceyard Cottage team) for letting me cause daily mayhem without (too much) complaint and for legging me up on Airgusta, Jason Cook for his kindness, skill and stopwatch, Roddy Llewelyn for calmness in an emergency and kindness afterwards, Graham Fletcher for finding Ballywhat, Charles and Merrigan Norwood for making me welcome in a strange place, Stephen and Karen Slack for their encouragement, Andrew Balding,

Henry Daly and Jamie Osborne for letting me disrupt their otherwise seamless operations, Georgie Browne for legging me up on Mr Music Man and Hayley, Gary and Jayne Moore for legging me up (twice for one race) on Theatre of Life.

Thanks also to Brian Lawson for his insistence that I try to deliver a "motivational speech" and to Yann Martel for inspiring 'the Tiger'.

I am extremely grateful to the people who contacted me after seeing a Taming Tigers presentation and agreed to have their stories included in this book. Thank you to Murray, Peter, Christine, Isobel, Paul, Katrina, Chris, Steve, Lotta and Catherine, our 'case study' contributors, for their time, effort, and honesty.

Nothing could happen in the Taming Tigers world without Aly Pendlebury who has brought this book together and Gerry Lawless who looks after our online presence and our studios so professionally.

A special thanks is due to Richard Dunwoody for all of his help and support along the way and for being kind enough to write the Foreword to this book.

Finally, I would like to thank Gee Bradburne (née Armytage) for all of her time and energy and pure hard work — in all weathers — to make it happen and both Gee and Maddie for their unswerving faith.

Foreword

Taming Tigers is an important book. Life is for living — and living well. Taming Tigers is all about setting ourselves free to do just that — at work or at home.

Taming Tigers is the antidote to 'self-help'. For one thing, the approach is completely practical. If you follow the Ten Rules you'll find very few 'short cuts' and no 'mantras' but a lot of excitement and challenge and opportunities to surprise yourself. But also Jim lives the philosophy. He doesn't just talk about it.

I rode nearly 2000 winners during my career including success in two Grand Nationals and a Cheltenham Gold Cup. I still hold the record for the number of racecourse falls — six hundred and seventy-two! Every day I rode there were Tigers to be tamed but nothing compared with the Tigers that attacked when I was told by an American kinesiologist, out of the blue, that my career was over. After seventeen years working on a racetrack, I was immediately running a business — sat in an office for twelve hours a day.

That was a far bigger personal challenge than riding Desert Orchid around any racecourse.

Facing change, whether we choose it or it chooses us, is a huge test but also a huge opportunity. And the battle is won or lost in our heads. This book unravels that battle.

Racehorses are a handful. And the few people who make it to ride in public on a racecourse have generally worked for many years with easier animals before they take a racehorse on. Their highly strung nature, coupled with their strength and speed, makes sitting on their backs, even on the gallops, an acquired taste. There is no brake, just 'negotiation' and if they decide they've had enough of you, more than likely you're off!

When I first heard about this guy from London who had arrived in Lambourn and was falling off and being run away with around the neighbourhood, I didn't fancy his chances. When Jim got in contact and asked me to help I couldn't resist and it was great to help him set his own record — fastest jockey from non-rider to track — and to be part of proving Taming Tigers.

Jim and I were lucky. We left the racing world without injuries that affect our lives. Not everybody is so lucky. Also, we — perhaps like you — enjoyed as children the good heath that permits us to get involved in sport. Racing Welfare (looking after people in difficulties in racing) and Sparks (medical research into childhood illnesses) are both benefiting from the sale of Jim's book and you can read about their work at the back of this book.

Early in 2008, to support Sparks, Racing Welfare and another charity close to my heart, Spinal Research, Doug Stoup, an American guide, and I completed a route from the coast of Antarctica to the Geographic South Pole that had only been completed in tractors and Sno-cats some fifty years ago. We became the seventieth and seventy-first people to reach the South Pole un-resupplied and without animal, machine or wind assistance. Our expedition was, without doubt, the toughest challenge I have ever taken on.

Having seen Jim speak a few weeks before I left the UK, I had his voice and Rule 10 ringing in my ears as things began to get really tough as we neared the Pole.

I'll be continuing to attempt to Tame my Tigers and I wish you every success with Taming yours. Rule 1 — Act boldly today. Who knows where it could lead you!

Richard Dunwoody MBE
Three Times Champion Jockey, Polar Explorer
Speaker and Author

Introduction

The Ten Rules for Taming Tigers is a re-structuring and a re-statement of truths that you already know. I didn't invent them, but I did observe them, experience them and experiment with them. And I have done my best to prove them by putting myself in a tricky spot with only the Ten Rules for company. I've now put them into a guide book which I hope is useful to you and gives the adversary in our heads a name — 'the Tiger'.

Having had the privilege of being invited to speak about them around the world, at the time of writing, some seventy thousand people have heard about the Rules for Taming Tigers in a conference room. Many of them have now experienced and experimented with the Ten Rules themselves. You can read some of their stories in this book. We are creating a Hall of Fame at www.tamingtigers.com for Tiger Tamers around the planet who have used these Rules to create exciting change for themselves and those around them. I find these stories the most compelling evidence that we're on to something worthwhile here.

This is not a book about riding horses at speed, wonderful though that is. The stories from my journey to the racetrack are simply there to illustrate how powerful these little Rules are and to give you confidence that each and every one was understood, tested and refined before being written down and passed on to you. To add to that confidence, I am delighted to be able to include case studies written by people who were in a Taming Tigers audience or who came across the Ten Rules in other ways. We have carefully and intentionally chosen case studies from people who have done real personal battle with the Tiger rather than big business case studies because, at heart, that is what this book is about.

If you would like to join with others from all walks of life who are working with these Ten Rules then please become a friend of Taming Tigers on Facebook. There, if you wish, you can state what it is you are going to take on or to change, you can ask for assistance and inspiration, share things that you have discovered or simply watch and bide your time.

There is another page dedicated to acknowledgments but this introduction would not be complete without stating that I didn't get to the racetrack alone. The Ten Rules caused me to meet some extraordinary people. Those people, along with the Rules, got me racing.

Tiger taming never stops, of course. So I wish you every success with taming your Tigers and I hope you'll wish me the same with mine. Please tell us about your experiences to help us improve the Rules and to encourage others to make the leap.

Jim Lawless
Dahab
2008

Table of Contents

Part One — Tigers and Racehorses   1

Chapter 1   What is a Tiger?   3

Chapter 2   The Ten Rules for Taming Tigers   15

Chapter 3   The Birth of Taming Tigers and a Bet   33

Part Two — The Integrity Rules   43

Chapter 4   Rule 1: Act boldly today — time is limited!   45
    Case study: Murray Elliot   63

Chapter 5   Rule 2: Re-write your Rulebook —
    challenge it hourly   67
    Case study: Peter Winters   83

Chapter 6   Rule 3: Head in the direction of where you
    want to arrive, every day   87
    Case study: Christine Lea   112

Part Three — The Leadership Rules   115

Chapter 7   Rule 4: It's all in the mind   117
    Case study: Isobel Ryder   136

Chapter 8   Rule 5: The tools for Taming Tigers
      are all around you   139
   Case study: Paul Croft   154

Chapter 9   Rule 6: There is no safety in numbers   157
   Case study: Katrina Dunkley   164

Part Four — The Change Rules   167

Chapter 10   Rule 7: Do something scary everyday   169
   Case study: Chris Pierce   187

Chapter 11   Rule 8: Understand and control your
      time to create change   191
   Case study: Steve Holliday   216

Chapter 12   Rule 9: Create disciplines — do the
      basics brilliantly   219
   Case study: Lotta Vilde Wahl   230

Part Five — The Esteem Rule   233

Chapter 13   Rule 10: Never, never give up!   235
   Case study: Catherine McDerment   250

Afterword   253

My first race   253
About the Author   265

About Sparks and Racing Welfare   266

Sparks   266
Racing Welfare   266

Part One

Tigers and Racehorses

Chapter 1

What is a Tiger?

You are writing the story of your life. You must be, mustn't you? Who else can be holding the pen?

If we have the good fortune to be healthy and to live in a free state rather than a dictatorship, we're pretty much writing the story. In the developed world, we have the privilege and luxury at this unique point in our history of being completely in charge of our own stories, with tremendous opportunity all around us. For economic benefit, yes, but also for intellectual, social, cultural and personal advancement and adventure.

So why don't we use that privilege fully?

We have a Tiger. All of us have a Tiger. The Tiger is the thing that stops us; roars at us when we consider doing something that will require us moving into unknown waters. We know we can justify intellectually why we do not move past the impasse. We can list the reasons why we should not do it. We never, of course, refer to it as our Tiger. We never allow others to see that we are actually justifying a lack of action caused by fear. Fear of the unknown. Fear of getting it wrong.

Let me illustrate. I was facing a huge Tiger in 2003 having been persuaded, against my better judgment, to deliver an 'inspirational presentation'. Until that point, I had presented on my areas of professional expertise only. This was a big departure. How dare I stand in front of a group of intelligent adults and 'inspire' them? Who the hell was I?

But my persuader, a man by the name of Brian Lawson, was a talented persuader and I gave in. As the phone call ended, my regret at agreeing began. I had three months.

Two months later, with four weeks to go, I'm beginning to have sleepless nights. I decide to book some time away with my partner and, at the airport, pick up a copy of "Life of Pi" by Yann Martel. It absorbs me and I've read it twice by the time I come home five days later.

A young Indian boy and his family decide to move their zoo from Pondicherry in India to Canada by sea. During a dreadful storm the freighter is sunk, and the only survivors are Pi and an adult male Bengal tiger, Richard Parker. Pi is no fool, he lives in a zoo. He knows that he will die either at the hands of the sea, if he gets out of the lifeboat, or at the hands of the tiger, if he stays in it. But then he begins to wonder, he begins to take action, he begins to make choices. He begins to change his rules about how the world works and decides to see if he can create new rules. He looks around him for anything he can use to help him. He abandons all the old ideas and relies only the new ones to help him in his new situation. He doesn't give up. He puts himself in scary, uncomfortable positions on a daily basis, but, months later, he is back on dry land and is safe.

I am inspired. I am wrestling with a Tiger in a little lifeboat called my head over this speech and the story inspires me to look at the situation afresh.

Then I wonder how many other people have a Tiger and I begin to canvass opinion. Everybody does. Taming Tigers is born.

Here is a question for you. When we are talking with our friends, telling them about what we would like to do with our lives — the great idea that we would like to see come to fruition, the plan of how we will make the family happy and peaceful, how we will do our bit for our communities, for our societies, even the planet — the plan, for many of us, simply to make more money. And when we see ourselves or our friends challenged to 'put our money where our mouth is,' why is it so rare that we do it?

Have you ever heard the cry, "What a great idea, you could do that!" and responded with a reply along the lines of:

- "Yes, of course, it's a great idea, and of course I can pull it off, but the wife/husband would never let me go for it";
- "The boss would never go for such a radical idea";
- "The mortgage would have to be cleared before I could think about doing that";
- "We could never afford it";
- "But that's not how we do it around here"
- "Not until the kids have left home";
- "Smarter men/women than me have tried and failed";
- "I'm too old";
- "I'm not clever enough"?

Well, unless you have had a long conversation with the wife/husband, approached the boss and gone through the business plan in some detail sat down with family and financial advisors to look pretty carefully at your next ten years' finances or found out whether it was their brains or their guts that got your heroes to where they are — *then you have met your Tiger.*

This book is not about 'success' in a traditional sense. It is not about making more money. It is not about having the perfect relationship. You can bet your life it's not about shortcuts and quick fixes and mantras that you can say to yourself in the mirror each morning to "manifest" love, wealth or happiness in your life.

You can use the Ten Rules for Taming Tigers for finding 'success' at home or work if that is what you wish to do, but that's not why I have become fascinated by the Rules and why I have tested them and now locked myself away to write them down.

This book is founded upon the belief that we all have a tremendous story to write, whether that story is about climbing mountains, making riches, creating world peace, bringing up some happy, contented children or playing a positive role in our communities. The question we start with here is not whether we have a great story to write or not. We all have the story in us. The question is whether we write our story or let the Tiger dictate it to us. You decide for you. I decide for me. That is what this book is about.

Let's look at this another way, I hope that one day I'll be a very happy, nimble old man. Ninety years old. I hope I'll be sitting in a nursing home somewhere watching the sea roll in and roll out. I hope that my life will be a little less frantic in those days, and that when I get up in the morning my biggest concerns will be: "Am I gonna win at cards today," and "Do I smell okay?"

There will be less paper left for me to write on, less ink left in the pen and I won't be writing so quickly in those far off days. What do I have to be doing today to ensure that when I look in the mirror at that old guy — after perhaps seventy or eighty years of pure opportunity, of being able to make choices, do things — I can smile at him and say to him, "Wow, we had some opportunities, we met some great people, we got out there, we made an impact, we made a difference, we wrote a story." It would be a real heartbreak in those distant days to have to look at the man in the mirror and think, "Wow, eighty years of possibility and we're still waiting for it to actually get started. What a terrible waste."

I believe deeply, through everything I've observed in others, studied or experimented with and experienced myself, that the difference between those who write that amazing story to look back on and those who live tormented and regretful in those late stages — or even still playing the deluded victim — is whether or not we tamed the Tiger. Whether, on a small, personal level of starting a conversation with a stranger or, on a large level in some commercial, social or political sphere, we were willing to take a risk that the Tiger wouldn't eat us as a result of doing something which was alien to us and which scared us.

But of course, this Tiger has no teeth. It only has a roar. If we can muster the courage to call its bluff, we walk straight past it. It's an illusion! A brilliant, powerful trick of the mind.

The Tiger is the thing that roars at you to keep your mouth shut when you're sitting in a meeting room with an amazing idea, that you are convinced will solve the problem — but feel too junior to speak out in this group. But it's your choice. It isn't a real tiger. These people aren't really going to eat you. The possibility of failure is pretty remote and the idea might be absolutely cracking if you think it through carefully. It is not the people, not the idea, not the culture, not anything else. It's just the Tiger that stops you from voicing the idea.

Salespeople are interesting — often full of Tigers. It is not the customer who forces the salesman to scale down his proposal, to be timid about the extent of problems that he could solve for his customer. The customer didn't do that. The culture of the salesman's own company and their mediocre targets and expectations didn't do that. The salesman did that.

The dreadful boss doesn't keep the brilliant, mercurial, dynamic youngster down. The youngster does (or doesn't). She creates her own rules about what she can or cannot do in this culture, what will and will not be acceptable, and can choose whether to comply and fit in with the gloopy culture of mediocrity that she sees in the organisation. But wait a moment, there is no rule that says that this culture had to be adhered to, that it can't be changed. And if she tires of trying to change it (that's genuinely trying to change it) then there is no rule that says that this young star should not move up and move on to a more stimulating organisation or culture within three/four months of realising that she cannot write her story in this environment. But maybe — and this is a thrill to watch — that youngster will stay. Stay and create something extraordinary within that organisation that nobody expected and nobody saw coming.

There is no rule that says we must live in unhappy relationships "because that's the role modelling I had as a child," or because "leopards don't change their spots," or because "he/she never listens to me anyway." It's the Tiger that stops us taking the risks necessary to find our way through these situations, to plan new and better lives with our partners or, if necessary, to find the strength to move on.

One story to create. One life.

Who's taking the choices? You or the Tiger?

So, again, what is a Tiger? The Tiger is that little nagging fear of failure and all the lovely little excuses we create in order to deal with it. Let me give you an example. I remember taking some air on a lovely summer's afternoon having delivered a presentation to a group of around a thousand people in Amsterdam. It seemed to have been well received. I had taken a few paces away from the walls of the conference centre to escape having to have a conversation with clouds of smoke drifting past me. But one of the guests at the event was particularly keen to say hello, and he followed me out onto the lawn. After saying some kind things about the presentation, he told me how jealous he was of me.

"Why?" I asked.

"Because I have always wanted to be a professional speaker and to inspire others for a living."

"No, you haven't!" I replied.

He looked stunned. "Yes, I have! I have always wanted to."

"No, you haven't." I replied. "If you had always wanted to do that for a living you would be doing it. You are doing exactly what you want to do for a living."

Now he was getting angry. Clearly, I was supposed to have massaged his ego on this.

"That's easy for you to say, you have a story to tell."

"Sure, but I didn't when I started speaking. And many speakers don't use their personal story — they are teachers and they have a philosophy or method to pass on that others find helpful."

"Yeah, but I guess it's different if you are a lawyer first and make your pile before taking a risk on speaking."

"Well, sorry to disappoint you, but I wasn't a good enough lawyer to have made any money by the age of twenty-nine, which is when I stopped!"

I gave him my number and an invitation to call whenever he wanted to ask me any questions on getting started in the career he had always wanted to pursue. He never called, of course. The Tiger ate his story for tea, poor guy.

If you truly believe that race, upbringing, religion, educational qualifications, gender, the mortgage, the wife/husband, the kids, the boss, the organisation you work for or the country you live in are the reasons why you are "unable" to do the things that you need to do, then you have a Tiger, and perhaps today is the first day of your life that you start being honest about it.

And let's face it. Don't you love that Tiger? Without it you would have to take the risk of getting on with the thing you should be getting on with or, even worse, admit thankfully to yourself that you're not big enough to start it. Face reality and let it go! But as long as the Tiger is there, you can keep yourself safe from such sleep-depriving thoughts.   .

It's not your fault.

And if you do tackle the Tiger, then I wish you success with all my heart. And you'll find a great many other people who tamed their Tigers will wish you the same success (check out Rule 5, 'The tools for Taming Tigers are all around you', to enlist their assistance). You will find a growing number of friends of Taming Tigers on Facebook who will wish you well and may even be able to assist you practically. Rule 1: 'Act boldly today — time is limited'. So come and state on our Facebook Wall precisely what you are going to do and what your first action is going to be.

If you do tackle the Tiger, you will find that it will attack you at moments of pressure, and you will need to learn how to handle this (Rule 4, 'It's all in the mind'). You will find that the Tiger in other people and their life's mission of imposing their Tigers on others in order to feel okay about themselves will get in the way, and you'll have to look through what it is that they're saying to you (Rule 2, 'Re-write your Rulebook — challenge it hourly').

You will need to push back on others' unreasonable demands on you in order to create time to make the new thing happen, and this will require discipline (Rule 9, 'Create disciplines — do the basics brilliantly') and it will require a plan and a driving sense of purpose (Rule 3, 'Head in the direction of where you want to arrive, every day') in order to bring it off. You'll have to look at your time as your truly scarce resource. You'll have to look at how you invest it and what return you want on that investment and face the Tiger of telling others that they cannot have what they want of you (Rule 8, 'Understand and control your time to create change').

You'll have to face the criticism that is always attracted to somebody trying to do something new and brave and bold, and learn to be comfortable with that criticism, enjoy that criticism, and even see it as a mark that you are now on the right path (Rule 6, 'There is no safety in numbers'). You will need to accept small personal risks and large risks alike as an acceptable part of your daily quest to do the right thing, and to begin with that may be unusual, so practice working on the risk muscle — trying new things that prove that it's only the Tiger standing in the way. (Rule 7, 'Do something scary every day').

So these Rules for Taming Tigers are not a map book to success. There is no such thing on any bookshelf, whatever they claim. These Rules for Taming Tigers will not 'reprogram your mind.' Would you really trust anyone who said that they would? These Rules for Taming Tigers are not about claiming loudly "I believe!" at the end of a motivational event before walking on hot coals, only to find that you don't believe so much when the bombs of daily life and survival are exploding all around you. There's an adrenaline thrill to the coal walk, for sure. But the laws of physics determine whether our flesh burns, not our state of mind. Adrenaline thrills have a short life. We, thankfully, do not!

These Ten Rules are about getting it started *and getting it finished*, and feeling the true freedom that comes from pursuing your own sense of purpose, and the true satisfaction that comes from doing the right thing and, yes, perhaps achieving something extraordinary for yourself or for others along the way.

I do not believe that there are shortcuts. You will find none in this book. Every rule that is written here has been tested in the high-risk arena of fat lawyers becoming jockeys, and has been tested in the business world, and has been proven to work consistently, as the case studies in this book will help you appreciate and the testimonials from business leaders underscore.

In short, I do believe that there is 'gold in them thar hills' (whatever gold might mean to you, personally). And I do believe that it is there for you to go and collect. Whether you're willing to get up every day and dig for it, rather than sitting in front of the television? Well, we must each answer that for ourselves.

Chapter 2

The Ten Rules for Taming Tigers

Time for the good news: Once you learn to recognise when you are taking the decisions and when the Tiger is, things get very exciting. Now is the opportunity to set yourself free and the only purpose of the Ten Rules is to help you to do that.

Now for the bad news: The Ten Rules do not contain shortcuts to wealth, health or happiness. Neither the Ten Rules nor I can 'make you thin', 'make you self-confident' or 'make you rich'. But then I doubt anybody else has actually achieved that for you have they? You probably did. Or you didn't.

And that is what the Ten Rules for Taming Tigers is for. With their help you can do it for yourself. No guru required! And that is the only way it was ever going to be possible. And that is also a lot more exciting and a lot more likely to have a long term success.

As we work together over the next hours, days or weeks, you will begin to understand the Tiger that you and your experiences have created much more closely than you do at this stage. As we do that, you will also begin to see the damage that the Tiger is doing and, I hope, to become angry.

Yes, I did say 'angry'. It's not a taboo emotion. Understood and used well, it can be a tremendous springboard for a new chapter and a new approach. As you begin to see the effect of the Tiger on the years that have passed so far — the story that has been written to date, however fabulous and successful it is — you will see areas, perhaps only small but perhaps very significant, where the Tiger has dictated and you have diligently written what it commanded. And that will create an emotion.

The overriding emotion for you may well be pride and joy at what a great job you have done of escaping the demands of the Tiger. It may be a shock to discover the extent of its impact on your life and that it has created the position that you now find yourself in — the sum of thousands of Tiger-driven decisions each year. In either case, some anger at the missed opportunities will be fine. It is that that drives the change.

The most important step so far, however, is to realise that you are in control. Nobody else is writing the story unless you live under an oppressive regime. You and your Tiger are therefore accountable for the story that has been created. And a good story changes direction in a single sentence.

Let's start writing!

The Rules are placed in an order and they are in that order for a reason. But they do not make up a linear process. That is important to grasp. These are not 'steps to success'.

In time, you will learn that in a tricky Tiger infested moment you may go with whichever of the Rules helps you. For now, though, read through them and begin to act upon them in the order in which they are written

The Rules, and the remainder of this book, are divided into four Parts:

- The Integrity Rules: Rules 1, 2 and 3
- The Leadership Rules: Rules 4, 5 and 6
- The Change Rules: Rules 7, 8 and 9
- The Esteem Rule: Rule 10

Let's have a look at each of the Parts

The Integrity Rules

Integrity n. Wholeness; soundness; steadfastness.

The Integrity Rules do not mean I'm suggesting you lack integrity in the usual sense. They are asking you to look at whether you act in integrity with what you want to do, what you would like to do, or what you believe that you could and should do. Are you working towards or living the kind of life that you would like to be living?

Rule 1: Act boldly today — time is limited

Rule 1 will ask you to get started. Not plan it. Not Google it. Not buy a book or talk to your friends about it. But to start it. And to start it like you mean it.

And whether you are the Chairman of the Board or studying for your first exams, when I ask you to start it like you mean it, you will have to confront why you haven't so far, and you'll meet the Tiger when you really, honestly consider doing it now. And that is where the integrity process begins. When you lure the Tiger out of the long grass and into the open and take a long look at him, perhaps for the first time, you will realise how well you know him, although you hadn't spotted him. You'll realise how closely you have lived together for all of these years in apparent harmony. And you'll gasp at how much of your story has been dictated to you by the Tiger. And you'll realise, when you look carefully, that you made him all by yourself.

And dare to wonder, my fellow Tiger tamer, what adventures might begin if you dared to begin the task of taming him. Today!

Seeing the Tiger and completing a bold action in accordance with the way that you, free of Tigers, truly want to act is the first step to seeing — or perhaps, feeling — the extent to which you are out of integrity with yourself. And the first step to finding that integrity again.

Rule 2: Re-write your Rulebook — challenge it hourly

Rule 2 confronts you with some of your very favourite strategies for remaining out of integrity with yourself. Your rational, carefully crafted, intellectually justifiable nonsenses. Nonsenses shared perhaps by millions, and almost certainly pandered to by friends and family alike.

Rule 2 demands honesty from you to yourself about the Tiger and the strategies that you are using to avoid meeting the Tiger: "I couldn't do it! My [insert restricting other, from bank manager to boss to spouse to parents] wouldn't agree to it." Is it them or the Tiger keeping you safe from taking a risk on writing a great story? Beginning to notice this, and learning strategies to overcome it, is the purpose of Rule 2.

Rule 3: Head in the direction of where you want to arrive, every day

Then we do some planning and take some steps along the road to only you know where. This is Rule 3. And this is still a part of the integrity process for two reasons.

First, Rule 3 is about committing to arriving at a place — and that gives a sense of purpose. It asks you to ask yourself what it is all about, where you want to go. Second, the planning is of real actions with real dates that will take you on a daily basis closer to being in alignment with the story that you want to be writing. This will also have you meeting the Tiger again and again as you make the space in your diary to write the story you should be writing.

Even as you reflect on how your time (your most precious and only truly scarce resource) must be spent differently to reach integrity you will have to confront the Tigers. Think about it. Every 'scary' conversation about what you could actually be achieving with a boss who gives you pointless tasks, every decision to ignore the bar and head home to work on creating a loving relationship has only been delayed up to today because of the Tiger you're feeding.

But integrity is only the starting place for our journey together, my Tiger taming friend. We are acting already, for sure, but only to hoist the sails and bring on provisions. Practical and real though those are, crucial steps though we will have taken, we'll need to sail our little craft when the skies darken and the waves crash over us to the jeers of our detractors. We'll need the second set of Rules for that.

The Leadership Rules

Leadership n. derivative of leader
Leader n. one who leads
Lead v. to be in charge; to influence towards action or belief;
    to draw a person or animal along

Don't worry. You do not have to be in a leadership position
to use the Ten Rules; although they will assist you to become
a better leader of others, whatever job title you enjoy. The
Leadership Rules, Rules 4, 5 and 6 are about taking the lead
in your own life. A precursor to taking the lead in anybody
else's. Having looked at the Integrity Rules and decided what
we must do and how we will go about it, it is time to take the
reins. It is time to take a lead, courageously, if necessary, in
your own life and in the lives of others. It is time to recognise
and defeat a whole new level of Tiger — the Tiger that our
interaction with others will unleash on us.

First, a word about leadership. The Ten Rules for Taming
Tigers were invented to assist leaders to lead when they were
'stuck' in delivering their (often more onerous) side of the
'change bargain' that they had struck with their people. By
that I mean that part when the new IT platform is installed,
the process consultants are about to withdraw and the leaders are required to risk leading the way in the behavioural
and cultural changes that will be the real decider in success.
So yes, the concept of leadership in industry has certainly
contributed to the growth of the Ten Rules and it has been
used by many leaders and delivered as part of several major
leadership programmes. 'Taming the Leadership Tiger' is a
presentation that I am often asked to deliver around the

world. So if you are in a position of leadership — or being asked to make that leap that is required of everyone these days of whatever rank or title — then the Rules will help you.

Whether you have any formal need to lead others or not, however, I would like you to stay with me on this. It is of vital importance. The shift to leadership over one's own life or 'being one's own person' is something that few people truly make. This is something that many older people recognise with hindsight and it is a weakness that those of them who fail view in themselves with regret. It is worthy of thought for the next five minutes or so, I assure you. You may even want to revisit it in a quiet moment in the car or train later.

For some people, becoming leaders in their own lives it is not an option that can be fully exercised in any event. Certain illnesses, extreme poverty or an oppressive regime snuff possibilities. Fortunately, for most of us, our biggest barrier is very probably the comfort of the developed world and its lack of urgency — our hunger for safety and predictability. How can we squander our freedom?

The ability to accept accountability for ourselves and to choose our own story and set about writing it, the integrity of knowing that our actions and decisions are guided by our carefully considered view of what is right and not by fear of making an error or of the harsh judgment of others, the commitment to purpose that gives us the right to inspire others and enlist them to our cause — these are the prizes that are on offer here.

When we are in control and not the Tiger, we are leaders of ourselves. We have the rudder, consciously, in our hands. And at that moment, strangely, we start to have a glimmer of the right to lead others about us. Strictly, that is another topic for another day, but the temptation to ask you to dwell on it with me for a moment is too great! Consider the classic leadership question: "What makes you think people would want to follow you?" Would the following play a part in your answer?

- The ability to take accountability for ourselves — to choose our own story and set about writing it rather than permitting fear in the moment to drive us off course (see Rule 4);
- The confidence to call upon others to assist us and inspire them to do so (see Rule 5);
- The integrity of knowing that our actions and decisions are guided by our carefully considered view of what the correct course of action should be and not by fear or the harsh judgment of others (see Rule 6);
- The ability to stand apart from the crowd, exposed, when required (but not for the sake of it) (Rule 6 again).

Any lack of the above would create early casualties in the leadership credibility race. Leadership 'behaviours' are surely dictated by an integrity, a 'state of mind', rather than a list in a textbook of observed traits. Rules 1–3 create that state of mind. Rules 4–6 maintain that state of mind under pressure from the Tiger and others and also help you to recruit others to help you tame your Tiger.

In our private lives we face the new level of Tiger attack that comes when we stand alone with our sense of purpose as our guide, when we need help but are intimidated by the Tiger from asking others and when the little voice of fear in our head is moving us away from integrity in our actions. In these moments, working with our Rulebook means creating a plan that begins to bring us back into integrity, preparing us to be the leader on that journey. Who will the leader be? Us? The Tiger? The opinion of others?

The Leadership Rules are also important in establishing your lead over the Tiger. It is here that the techniques are learned to move beyond recognising it to consistently defeating it.

Rule 4: It's all in the mind

So, in Rule 4 we will explore together practical tools and tips to keep your head when the chips are down and the Tiger is telling you that you should retreat rapidly or even surrender. We will also look at choosing your approach to situations and dealing with the setbacks and confidence blows that give the Tiger such strength as we move along our journeys.

Rule 5: The tools for Taming Tigers are all around you

Rule 5 is a very powerful Rule. The recognition that whatever we would like to achieve, the tools and, most of all, the people that we need to get us there are already sitting waiting to help us. But we may need to deal with a few major Tigers before we are open enough to permit their assistance. Here we examine the shift from 'dependence' to 'independence'. Then we go for the stretch — how many of us will attain 'interdependence' and really get results? But none of that will hold the power it should without Rule 6.

Rule 6: There is no safety in numbers

Now the 'C' word begins to become a little more evident: 'Courage'. How well is the Tiger managing to stop us being our own person in action, striking out in the direction we believe to be right despite the calls from the crowd to return? Calls that have been ground into us from school days and before and are repeated every day by marketing moguls and mediocre managers.

"Stick with the crowd! Run with the pack!" So the Tiger roars at us, far louder than the actual pack does. They are generally too busy wondering what to eat for tea to care that much about us, but they will make a reflex reaction and fulfil their duty to display their wisdom to us, for sure.

And when they do call us back, and we do not want to return, that is scary. Which is why Rule 7 has been one of the most important Rules for Tiger tamers for the past five years. And why it is the first of the Change Rules. But let me introduce you to the Change Rules before we take on Rule 7. Isn't 'change' just an overused business term? Undoubtedly! But don't let that put you off of its scent.

The Change Rules

Change v. tr. to make different; to swap; to refresh
Change v. intr. to undergo alteration

So, we shall take accountability and responsibility and learn that only the Tiger is in the way of us writing our story. We shall take actions and re-evaluate our Rulebook. We will have a plan. We'll be able to cope when the going gets tough. We'll work with others to get a new level of outcome but we'll stand alone when we need to.

What more could we want?

Consolidation and consistency. We want to stay in the exciting new place, even move forward from it! We want to create a long term change and not a momentary flash of inspired action. We need the next three Rules, the Change Rules.

Do people want to give up smoking for a while or consolidate the achievement and be consistent in not smoking ever again? Do they want to lose weight just for the summer or consolidate and consistently live at a lighter weight? Do they want to inspire the team at the next monthly meeting or consolidate and consistently be an inspiration to the team?

Do you want to tame this Tiger and take some exciting decisions and actions about this story that you're writing that will disappear in a few pages, or do you want to move your experiences onto a whole new level?

My pleasure at reading an email from an audience member or seminar attendee who tells me that they "finally did it!" they "finally plucked up the courage to do that bungee jump at the beginning of that James Bond film — and all thanks to recognising their Tiger" is immense.

The other email that comes, often years after an event, is the reason that I do what I do. This email tells me that, having decided that the Tiger was all that held her back from presenting at work (she had never delivered one for this reason), she has taken training and practiced over the last eighteen months. She has taken bolder and bolder risks in the boardroom. She now stands in the centre of the room with authority and even turns the slides off from time to time. She secures budget for the projects that she and her team believe are important and her team are becoming ever more loyal to her as a leader. She has been promoted several times and is now thinking about accepting an invitation to speak at trade events.

She, or he, will always end the email with a version of this sentiment: "The strange thing is, it's not just [whatever their challenge was], it's everything. I'm just more confident and not afraid to be me".

That consistent consolidation of Tiger taming is the value of the Change Rules, Rules 7, 8 and 9.

Rule 7: Do something scary every day

In case you hadn't noticed, this is a book about how we deal with our reaction to risk. I believe that our perception of, and reaction to, risk determines a great deal of our story. These Rules are designed to help us take better decisions around risks. We'll deal with this in much more detail later in the book but, think about it for a moment now — your reaction to risk is important. As an example, your reaction to risk is likely to determine who you will meet and speak to in life. It is likely, therefore, to directly influence the genetic makeup of your children! Get the point? Good. Let's get cracking before it's too late.

Rule 7 is about simply flexing the risk muscle, flexing the Tiger taming skills on a daily basis, working on it intentionally in comparatively safe environments, feeling how it works on us and coming through in one piece. This enables us to write a new rule for the Rulebook about 'risk'. It enables us to grow in confidence. And it makes the Tiger easier to recognise; easier to tame.

But that won't do the job alone. We will need a whole new relationship with time if we are to consolidate the change and make Tiger Taming a new habit, a way of life.

Rule 8: Understand and control your time to create change

Rule 8 is not about 'time management'. We have a deep relationship with time. We rarely examine this relationship and very often it is unhealthy. When we reach Rule 8, it is time to be sure that yours is thriving. Once we have a healthy relationship with the concept of time, it is possible to exert control over it. Once we exert control over our time, we can begin to create a consistently Tiger-free way of thinking.

What is the one scarce resource that you have to invest in your future? Really? If you run out of money, what can you do about it? If you run out of oil, what alternatives will there be? And when you run out of time, what'll you do then?

We don't 'spend' this scarce resource doing things. We invest it doing things. It always brings a return. A life spent watching daytime TV, eating pizza and drinking whisky is invested — it brings a very definite return.

What's your investment plan?

And if you're investing your time in writing a great story — the story that you have chosen and that will have you leaping out of bed tomorrow with a mixture of excitement and trepidation — you'll find Rule 9 a great help to you.

Rule 9: Create disciplines — do the basics brilliantly

Olympic athletes have rules for themselves. They have rules about training, rules about diets, rules about mental toughness and, usually, rules about the order in which they will put their kit on.

Discipline is not a sexy word for most people. We'll not be looking at the disciplines that you may have found frustrating at school or the disciplines (bureaucracy) that may seem to impede you at work. We're talking about the thrilling basics that, once you have identified, uniquely, for yourself, you can practice and rely on when times are tough; when you are out there alone.

What is the one thing that, if you did it consistently brilliantly every single day, would make the biggest impact on your chosen story in twelve months?

Think about it. We'll come back to that.

The Esteem Rule

Esteem v. tr. to regard favourably
Esteem n. positive regard

Over the years, Rule 10 has become known as the Esteem Rule.

Now, I am not a psychologist but you and I have both noticed that esteem can be built through achieving things that we set out to achieve and that we're proud to have achieved. This does not, in my view, have to be an achievement like becoming President of our nation or winning gold at the next Olympic Games; it can be as simple as buying the fresh ingredients for, and then preparing, a nourishing meal for our family or friends and ourselves. That's a decent enough achievement in most people's twenty-first century schedule.

To achieve something, we have to *do* things and we have to *finish* them. That is, we have to carry on doing things until the thing is complete. There is no achievement in a fridge full of rotting ingredients. And as the magnet on the front of that fridge may remind you, "Fear is temporary. Failure is forever".

This is another area where Taming Tigers diverts heavily and determinedly away from traditional 'self-help'. There's a lot more courage and sweat than 'shortcut' and 'mantra' required to tame a Tiger, but the result is the more exciting for it as Tiger tamers around the world, myself included, have discovered and are discovering. You'll soon get to read some of their stories.

So, the first part of esteem building is the doing of things. Not the planning of things, not the saying of things (unless this act achieves a result in itself — cheering somebody up, for example), not the writing down of things, not the discussing of things, not dreaming things and not hoping that a reality TV show will eventually deliver your hearts desires. It is the doing of things. All of the Rules — from Rule 1 to Rule 10 — deal with this dreadful thought: You have to get out there and do things. But once you learn to recognize and tame the Tiger, it's great and highly addictive!

The second part is keeping going until it's done. And that's the rub, isn't it? Maybe we, too, "could have been a contender", but the thing of it is that "could have" means we stopped. And the Tiger will set up many, many opportunities under many, many guises for us to stop.

When I first started working with the Ten Rules for Taming Tigers, there was no Rule 10. I thought that I had it covered in eight Rules back then. But during the racing year I learned something from myself and the other athletes whom I met:

Only dogged determination not to be beaten will get you through the really bad days when the Tiger throws the whole damn lot at you.

All of the other Rules are too subtle in this vital and deadly phase of combat with ourselves. The Tiger is too wily in how it makes us view our position as we angle for an exit route that we can justify. Dogged persistence is the only thing that is going to get you to a position where you might be able to finish the thing you set out to finish, write the chapter of your story that you set out to write and collect the esteem bonus as a result.

And that required a Rule, so Rule 10 was born:

Rule 10: Never, never give up

Why? Because failure has a consequence that keeps out of sight when savage battle rages in our heads but that we carry with us forever: Loss of self-esteem and loss of confidence. The failure bonus.

The Ten Rules for Taming Tigers

So, now we are all introduced, let's get stuck in and start getting even more excited about being alive than you already were when you bought this book. And here are the little devils that will deliver that for you or I'll eat my horse's breakfast.

1. Act boldly today — time is limited!
2. Re-write your Rulebook — challenge it hourly
3. Head in the direction of where you want to arrive, every day
4. It's all in the mind

5. The tools for Taming Tigers are all around you
6. There is no safety in numbers
7. Do something scary every day
8. Understand and control your time to create change
9. Create disciplines — do the basics brilliantly
10. Never, never give up!

Chapter 3

The Birth of Taming Tigers
and a Bet

Part I — "Bring out your dead!"

7.30am, regular as clockwork, Richard walks in to the office. I know this by reputation; I've never been in this early before. But today I'm behind so I'm sitting, invisible to anybody else, in my cordoned-off 'pod' in the open-plan office of the IT multi-national where I am an International Legal Counsel. Richard lets out a large groan and says, to the empty office he sees "Oh, well, only four years, two months, three weeks and two days to go." I stop working on the contract and do a quick calculation on the back of an envelope. I reckon I've got thirty four years, six months, two weeks and three days to go. And that's if I'm lucky enough to be able to afford to retire at sixty-five.

The office block where we all work in Slough is conven-ient for the motorways of the UK and for London's Heathrow Airport, but for little else. I would never have guessed it, but it did me the biggest favour in my life. My desk was by a window on the ground floor, next to a side-street that led up to a much bigger road at the front of the office. Somewhere, I didn't hang around long enough to find out exactly where, there was a funeral parlour. And every morning as I started work the hearses would start coming past me carrying their loads. And by lunchtime they would return empty. This, coupled with my friend Richard prompting my calculating that I had nearly thirty-five years of my sentence yet to run, got me thinking. "What if this actually is as good as it gets?"

The genie was let out of the bottle. If this was my life, what on Earth was I going to do with it? When was it going to get started? Maybe it already had.

That lunchtime, I went to the library in Slough for the first time. There they had a computer programme to tell you what careers you could be suitable for. It recommended that I should think about being a forensic scientist, a landscape gardener or a photographer. I liked the sound of photographer but would I make any money at it? (notice the Tiger at work). The following Sunday I was to fly to Bucharest to take a part in the negotiation of a major government contract that we were to fulfil there. On the way, I picked up a book someone had lent me some time before, "The Year Of The King" by Antony Sher. As I sat high above the clouds, looking forward to an early Monday start in our Bucharest office, I reached a description written by Sher of his transformation from himself into his portrayal of Tartuffe and his entry onto the main stage at London's Barbican theatre. Oh, how I envied the skill, the emotional thrill, the self-reliance and the pure adventure of it! I sat in my seat and I dreamed, and I cursed the rotten luck that destined me to be a lawyer and not a stage actor! But by the time I landed in Bucharest I'd got over myself and decided that, seeing as I wasn't going to be a landscape gardener, I would go and find out what Sher felt like. I had no big desire to spend the rest of my life being an actor, but I decided it would be quite an adventure to find out what it was like to walk out onto the stage.

And so it was time for some of the boldest, bravest things I had ever done. By that September I was enjoying my first day at Guildford School of Acting as a drama student. Without a doubt, the most important personal and professional learning year I experienced until taking my riding bet. Whilst at Guildford, I experienced what Antony Sher had described (though, I confess, not at the Barbican), and on leaving Guildford, although I established my change company, Optimise straightaway, I also took the odd acting job and thoroughly enjoyed working on a few film-sets and in some small theatre tours.

Part II — Never say never . . .

Optimise was initially all about bringing performance skills to business people — helping people inspire their audiences rather than clubbing them with tedium (as I had done for many years). I felt I understood the worlds of performance and business now and, before long, large companies felt that my team were good at helping them inspire their people and we evolved, through study and experience into 'change' experts, inspiring people in big organisations to see how things could be better, and how it was worth the personal risk of trying.

I loved the work and was soon honoured to be invited to give presentations on change or communications at various corporate events. Then, one fateful day, the telephone rang and I was invited to give a motivational presentation. I immediately refused. I thought that loud razzmatazz 'American-style' speeches were an appalling idea; I had nothing to speak about in any event; and I was terrified!

Well, the caller, a man called Brian Lawson who worked for a global telecoms company that was a client of ours, was not to be refused. He'd already sold the idea of me addressing the event to his boss and he wasn't about to back down. So, after several calls and having my confidence boosted by Brian's persuasion skills, I accepted the job. I had three months to prepare.

As we have discovered, Yann Martel's "Life of Pi" came to my rescue and I wrote to Yann Martel immediately on my return to see if he would be happy for me to use the Tiger metaphor.

What was the thing that had kept me at a lawyer's desk looking at contracts for many (for me, personally) unhappy working years? What was the Rulebook I was living by that said that this was how it had to be? Why was I so terrified of taking bold steps into the unknown? Was it really likely that I would come to physical or even long-term financial harm? Of course not.

It was the Tiger.

I was also aware that this was a new way of articulating principles that had for a long while underpinned the work that Optimise had been doing in change and in communications training. We had been helping individuals to change the

Rulebook and to have the courage to take action. We'd been helping them create a plan to a new place and work with others to get there. It worked!

And the more I considered it, the more I was convinced that we all had a Tiger — the thing that stops us, roars at us when we try to do things which are new or scary or have a risk attached to them for us.

Speech day comes and I am to deliver sixty minutes of motivational genius. After thirty minutes I thank the audience and bow to their slightly surprised applause. I had become pretty adept at speaking on subjects where I'm an expert. Even delivering a Shakespearean monologue was something that I'd have felt comfortable with. However, delivering sixty minutes of motivational material to a couple of hundred senior and experienced sales guys seems to have beaten me. I've been in such a nervous state that I have missed out clumps of material — all carefully timed at home to meet the required hour and beautifully crafted — and I'm standing mute with thirty minutes left to go. The host is kind enough to call an early coffee break and save his dismay for a private moment later. But to my amazement, as I try to leave with a feigned smile on my face, one of the audience members approaches me, says how much she enjoyed it and asks if I would polish it up and deliver it again a month later.

At that event things go slightly better, until the end. There are to be questions and answers. One of the questions comes up: "What have you ever done to tame your Tigers, Jim?"

I attempt a bold reply about leaving Law, going to drama school, setting up my own business and even standing up on a stage today, but my world-weary questioner is singularly unimpressed.

"We're constantly innovating, we're constantly going into bigger and scarier sales situations and you're standing up there telling us about taming our Tigers. What you're really talking about here is looking at our deepest, darkest fears and overcoming them."

I don't really like the direction this conversation could be taking. My problem, of course, is that a couple of hundred guys in the room are loving the direction that this conversation is taking.

My interrogator continues, "So, I've got a little challenge for you, to see whether your Taming Tigers has any value to it. If you don't mind my saying, you are quite a short bloke." I do mind this, but my Tiger is roaring quite loudly, so I stay quiet, the blood draining from my face.

"And if you don't mind my adding, you are slightly overweight." I really do mind this, but see above quandary.

"So I'm gonna bet you that you can't become a jockey riding in a televised race under official Jockey Club rules within twelve months. In fact I'll bet you a pound that you can't."

I'm hoping that nobody notices that I'm gripping quite hard to the lectern to stay upright at this point. I manage to take a deep breath and sound convincing and vaguely adult when I reply that that's a ridiculous idea as I've only sat on ahorse a couple of times, both of them pony-trekking as a kid, and on both occasions the horse won a convincing victory over me.

His face breaks into the kind of evil smirk that the 'baddies' have in the movies when they realise that they have the upper hand on the 'hero'.

"In that case, it will be a really interesting Tiger to tame, won't it?"

My mind is flashing through scenarios. In a moment, I have thought about my diary, my family, the opportunity to really put some credibility around the Ten Rules, and what a great adventure it would be, all punctuated by visions of falling off horses. Could it be done?

I leave the stage without saying anything and walk over to his table. I extend my hand saying that I agree on the condition that I can have one month's prep time to put a plan in place.

He nods and we shake hands. A new adventure.

Part III — Reality Check

On the way back home that evening I'm feeling pretty good. I've taken on a challenge to prove the integrity of the principles that I've been using to underpin my work in change and that I've now started spouting on stage in front of some pretty impressive people. It wouldn't do me or the Rules any harm to be put to the test. And anyway, when I left Law I decided that life would be an adventure. And here I was. I had left the house an overweight businessman off to give a presentation to a bunch of sales guys, and I was coming home a man who had just over twelve months to be riding in his first televised horserace.

You never can tell what a difference a day will make!

But there was a flip side to this which was beginning to create butterflies in my stomach as I sat on the train home. Those readers who might think that, by thirty, a lawyer is made for life are taking a slightly rosy view of a young lawyer's income. There was nothing much in the bank — drama school and setting up Optimise had put paid to any savings. Of course, you'll be thinking, he must have had connections in horseracing. Nobody can get into horse-racing without connections!

Sadly, no. Not one. I'd been brought up in a place called New Malden, in South London. Not many horses about. And certainly no racing stables. I went to a large London comprehensive (state) school and there were no stables there either. In fact, to tell the truth, I'd been to the races twice in my life. On both occasions it had been in a corporate hospitality area, and on both occasions I'd enjoyed the hospitality just a little too much to focus on the horses, and lost more money than I should have done with the bookmakers.

Maybe I had, in fact, bitten off more than I could chew.

But my spirits didn't really get rocked until I got home to my laptop and decided to learn a little bit about jockeys and their lives. I learn that they get up at 5am most mornings and are at work by around 6am. And, get this, they do that six days a week, twelve months of the year. That includes winter!

I learned that jockeys riding on the flat weigh out for races between seven and a half stone and nine and a half stone. Now, I didn't own weighing scales at this phase in my life. I did like beer and I loved takeaway food. And I had a dim recollection of having weighed in at around twelve stone the last time I had had a medical. I learned that jockeys are very fit. This came as a blow as I had thought that the horses would do all the work. I hadn't owned a pair of running shoes since I had been at school, and I had left school eighteen years ago.

Most worryingly though, I learnt that jockeys usually started riding horses somewhere between the ages of six months and twelve months. Try as I might, I couldn't find any stories of jockeys who had started learning to ride at thirty-five.

The Rulebook was working its magic. Beautifully designed to keep me safe, the Rulebook started to place rational sounding obstacles in my way. I had started a battle that would rage for the next year. The battle with the Tiger had begun.

Part Two

The Integrity Rules

Chapter 4

Rule 1: Act boldly today — time is limited

Let's cut straight to it, I believe that the most fundamental difference between those people who can look back from the nursing home thinking that they gave it their best shot, they wrote a story, and those who must look back and give the Tiger credit for dictating their story to them is that the first lot acted. They overcame their reticence to get stuff started.

And this, of course, sounds blindingly obvious. At this point even I would be thinking about getting this book back to the shop before I broke the spine. So let me ask you: if you think of the next big thing that you need to achieve and you think of the biggest, boldest action that you need to do in order to start the process or give the process some momentum, are you going to do that today? Think it through carefully before you take the book back. Now try and think of a bolder action, one that could really get you quickly to the objective, quickly to the end point you want, whether that's a business, personal or social thing that you want to achieve. What is the biggest and the boldest thing that you could do today to make it happen?

Now when you thought about doing that bold thing today — that's today, within the next thirty minutes, not tomorrow — did you meet a Tiger?

As soon as you start thinking, honestly, about the bold action that you know is the most direct and certain way to take you towards the thing that you want to achieve next, you will meet the Tiger. That is partly why acting boldly is Rule 1 — to get acquainted with him up close, to see what he smells like. If you win and take this next action then, however bold it may feel to you, I promise you will look back in twelve months and be amazed at what a small action it was.

If you don't take it, it will still be there as big and scary as it is today in a year, maybe a decade, dictated to you by the Tiger rather than written by your true self. Except, of course, there is no Tiger, is there? There's just you.

Have you done the bold thing? Have you put this book down already and done the bold thing?

Or are you doing some planning first? Thinking it through? Looking at the pros and cons? Talking yourself out of the big bold action, reducing it until it is no longer the big bold action it was but rather a little, but still mildly scary, action?

In my work in corporate change, doing 'the bold thing' and doing it 'today' was a tool that we often used to help people realise how much better they could be making things if they really wanted to. So it came as a real blow to me in the racing challenge, when I realised that I had learned nothing about this rule.

On the morning after researching my racing bet, I took my first bold action. I rang the only person in the world I knew with an interest in horseracing. A man called Stephen. I was quite edgy, so I rang him as early as I thought I could get away with (7.30am) and calmly announced that I had twelve months to become a jockey. After he'd finished spluttering on his muesli, I asked him what he thought it was like being a jockey.

"Well, I don't think you'll like it much."

"Why not?"

"Well, let me put it like this. Imagine you were standing on the seat of your motorbike, but the motorbike was about three times the size it is normally. Oh, and you're not allowed to hold on to the outside of the handlebars, you hold on to the middle of the handlebars. And then some character presses a button and the motorbike suddenly flies into action at around thirty miles an hour, with you holding on at the top."

"Hmm. Go on . . ."

"Well, after a while you'll need to speed this bike up to a faster speed as the race gets going."

"Do I?" I asked, doubtfully.

"Yes. So you start moving your backside up and down, pushing the handlebars hard with your hands, and then to really get things going you take one hand off (you're at about thirty-seven/thirty-eight miles per hour now) and wave one hand furiously behind you with a stick in it."

"That doesn't sound safe!"

"It's not."

"So what about Health & Safety regulations? They can't just let people go out and do dangerous things in front of an audience, this isn't Ancient Rome. Will I get a protective jacket, a full-face helmet and visor if I'm going to stand on the seat of my motorbike at that speed?"

"Nope. You get a silk jacket, which you wear over a very flimsy little body protector. You get a skullcap but that's not much help in a serious fall or if you get kicked."

"Kicked?"

"It can happen if you fall off, sure."

"Oh. So do I get a saddle with a safety-belt? How do you stay on this thing instead of hitting the deck if there's a collision at speed?"

"No. You don't want to be staying on it if there's a collision at speed. What you really hope is that you'll be thrown well clear!"

"Thrown? At what speed did you say?"

"Around thirty-eight miles per hour. But think about it. There might be fourteen horses each weighing half a ton, each bringing down that weight hard against the surface through four little legs which have got nasty, sharp metal shoes on, coming up behind you, and then you go and fall off. You want to be thrown as far away from that as possible."

"Do I?"

"Yep."

"Okay. Thanks, Stephen. Bye."

"Bye."

So that was a good conversation, then.

The Power of Acting

So the primary difference between those who can revel in the ultimate delight — the thrill of having done battle out there, having written a story, made a difference — and those who will have to face up to a story dictated by the Tiger is down to Rule 1. Acting. Doing something about it. Getting it started. Without that, there can be nothing.

But, and it is a big but, most of us act anticipating defeat. We act in a small way. We act as the Rulebook (see Chapter 5) tells us we "may" act, as it "permits" us to act. And we are likely to get a poor result from that. We need to act boldly, act like we mean it, to get a big bold helpful result. I had said this many times at work but now I was to learn it the hard way on the way to the racecourse.

But do *you* agree that this is the major differentiator? That this Rule, more than any other, will help us to defeat the Tiger and have a story that we can be proud of? A story without regrets? Well how many great ideas have you had that you see on the marketplace a few months or years after you had them? The difference isn't that "they were cleverer", that "they were rich" or that "they got lucky". The difference is that they did something about it.

And as soon as we consider doing something about it — a big bold thing, like we really mean it — the Tiger comes into play. The self-doubt and fears begin. The Rulebook kicks in. The little voices in our head begin. The sure knowledge that nobody would want to help *us*. The dreaded possibility of failure. All of the manifestations of the Tiger that we shall meet as we go through the Rules together will start off.

But doing something is so simple, the result so exhilarating and the possibilities of making a great change so high once it is done, that it becomes the first of the Ten Rules. That and the fact that it exposes the Tiger to you straight away so that you can have a look at the enemy and gauge his strength.

So, please, do something about it! Harness the tremendous power and energy that comes from doing something, from action. Once we take an action, nothing is ever the same again. Once we take an action, others are involved. Once we take an action, the dithering is over and possibly, just possibly, we will move towards a commitment. And once we have a commitment, our hearts have joined with our heads. Now, anything could happen.

And because we are now acting in line with what we *say* we want to achieve, rather than in line with what the Tiger dictates and the excuses that follow, it is the first Integrity Rule. When we act in integrity with ourselves rather than in fear of the Tiger, we have a chance of starting a new chapter in the story.

Now I began my working life as a lawyer, so getting it done today is a pretty counter-intuitive approach for me. We famously like to have a good think, write a letter, dictate a file note and then wait a bit. It may well be that in your area of professional expertise, rash unplanned actions would be frowned upon too.

So let's deal with that for a moment. When I asked you about the bold action, did your mind start to stray towards a bold, risky, rash deal that could bring down the company? Or did your mind wander off to something far more mundane but just as scary? The kinds of actions we are speaking about here are very rarely the kinds of things that could do us real harm. Clearly an unprofessional or reckless action is not what I am recommending, but do check in with the Rulebook here. Is what you are thinking about really a negligent action or does the culture just like to pretend that it is to excuse mediocrity?

Now, of course, you may well still be thinking that you have no Tiger to tame, you're pretty bold. So good for you. Before you leave the chapter, let's just check how Tiger-free you really are. Think of the boldest action that you could take to make whatever it is you want to achieve come closer to you. Now try harder. I didn't say the quite scary thing that you could do! I said the boldest.

Now use that imagination and try again. Now you're getting there.

Now do it. Now!

The excuses that you are coming up with are simply the Tiger. No, it's not too late in the day. Yes, you could find the number if you tried!

Congratulations. You are getting acquainted with it.

Now do it.

Stop diluting it and doing deals with yourself about what you will do tomorrow. Do it now. Tomorrow will not be easier. It'll be the same, but with the added gift of you feeling that you wimped out today.

How's the pulse?

Now do it.

Once that 'it' is done, feel free to turn over.

* * * * *

Congratulations. A Tiger has been tamed.

Or you have met one of the other ways that the Tiger affects you; something that provided you with a good excuse not to do the thing. If that's the case, you'll get it done before the end of this book. You'll soon meet the Rule that helps you with that particular Tiger attack.

Action before commitment

To me, this is the crux of it. This is where it all begins. This is perhaps the most important paragraph in the book! Commitment flows from the bold action. The bold action does not follow a moment of commitment.

Read that again. Have a little think. Do you agree?

Nothing happens without commitment. Or, to be more precise, nothing gets finished without commitment. Nothing. You will be committed to cooking a meal and satisfying your hunger. That's committed. You'll be committed to getting all the emails and voicemails dealt with so that nobody is giving you grief. That's committed. But you may not yet, for a number of reasons, be committed to writing what you really want to write in the next chapter of your story. And that is why it may look like you'll be writing what you wrote in the last chapter. Again.

There is a moment, a thrilling moment, which you may have experienced, when we commit. When we say to ourselves and maybe even to others, "This thing shall be done and I shall do it. I have no idea how. I have no idea what this decision will lead me towards, what I will have to do or who I will meet along the way but I, personally, shall make it happen." Maybe you made that commitment on your wedding day, maybe you made it when you saw your child for the first time, maybe you have made it in your studies or your career.

It is this moment that changes lives, changes our world. This is the moment that can even change the course of the entire world if you are an Alexander Fleming committing to bring penicillin to public attention or a Kennedy pledging to put a man on the moon. They were just people too. They had Tigers.

Commitment gets things done.

I now know that I did not commit to becoming a jockey when I took the bet. I committed a couple of weeks later. I thought that I had committed but I had not. I had burned no bridge, I had made no irreversible change, I had a reverse gear available.

The bold action brings people into the project. The bold action makes things immediately different. The bold action emboldens you to dare to dream that you could actually do the thing, write the chapter. The bold action permits you to speak your mind and seek true responses. The bold action gives you integrity and clarity and from there you may find yourself making that commitment. The bold action reveals your only dangerous adversary. Your Tiger.

Rule 1 at the races

A couple of days after my bet, I was attending a formal dinner. I found all twelve stones of me sitting next to a sprightly Sir Keith Mills, the founder of Air Miles and of Nectar, a great yachtsman and one of the architects of the London 2012 Olympic bid. He asked what I was up to as I tucked into a portion of trifle, so I told him. He began to chortle, then he realised that the idea of this twelve stone trifle-muncher being a jockey was so entertaining that he called the table to silence to tell everybody — a salutary lesson in my mouth writing cheques that my spirit seemed unlikely to actually cash.

"How long have you been riding?" one of the other guests fired back.

"I've been pony trekking twice." I answered. This really found their funny spots. I was keen for the speeches to start.

A year later, once I had had my first ride, I contacted Keith to tell him. He was generous in his congratulations and I was very pleased to remove the monkey that I had placed on my own back that evening. I had not intended my naive answer to Keith to be a bold action, but it turned out to be one and the reaction of the table helped me immensely.

So I acted boldly that evening by leaving the remainder of the trifle uneaten. That hurt! And I went on a diet from that moment on. I only ate fruit until lunch time, I refused all biscuits in meetings and I substituted dessert for a walk after my evening meal. This seemed radical at the time.

I also decided that evening that I would have to quickly face up to the other big scary truth. This "jockey" couldn't ride horses. In fact, the thought of getting onto a horse terrified me. During one of my pony trekking trips, one had got onto the ground whilst I was on its back — a bit like a camel might — and started to roll. I had hopped off as it went down and was shouting to the guide, who shouted back that I was an idiot to have let go of the reins and screamed at me to grab them quickly.

"Why?" I called back. But as my horse got up and bolted into the trees ahead, I cottoned on to the idea.

So as I nursed a beer later after the dinner and alternated between reliving my experience at the table and reliving the decision to jump off of the horse, I decided to book a lesson the following morning. I was feeling a bit clammy so I ordered another beer. It had not even dawned on me at that stage that my seventeen year old love affair with alcohol was under threat.

I rang the local riding yard and booked in.

"What are your riding goals?" they asked — an interesting start. I liked their style.

"I'm going to be riding under Rules on the racetrack in twelve months." I was booked in for the following day. I thought that I could detect a frisson of excitement as I arrived. The girls in the yard were clearly waiting for somebody interesting and they seemed to be mistaking me for him! I smiled back at them but they looked a little doubtful as I stepped out of my car. It occurred to me later that jockeys generally have a less full figure, and face, than I did. And that they wear riding kit rather than wellington boots and jeans.

I went into the office and announced myself.

"Aha!" declared my tutor, "We've all been looking forward to meeting you. Tell me what you have been doing. Where do you ride? Who do you know? Who has been teaching you?"

"No, No! It's my first day today!"

Her face fell and we stared at each other in silence for a few seconds.

I don't know the name of the animal I was supposed to ride. It has become "Trigger" in my mind. He let out a whinny of contempt as he was led back to his box and Dobbin was brought out to take his place. I was not certain whether

the whinny was aimed at me or at Dobbin, but I think I know
the answer. The girls got back to their jobs around the yard,
and I didn't get a wave goodbye after my lesson.

The following Friday I was in the pub with some friends.
I was often in the pub with some friends in those days. I was
tucking into my pie and pint (everybody knows that calories
don't count on a Friday). We were relaying the stories of our
weeks and, as I recounted mine, their eyes were widening. I
was certainly the centre of attention tonight.

"So tell us about these Ten Rules for Taming Tigers" they
asked. I told them.

"So, do you have to start with Rule 1?"

"Yes, but the rest are non-sequential."

"So what's the bold action you did?"

I told them about the trifle, the fruit, the biscuitlessness,
the walks and the riding lesson. They were clearly unimpressed.

"But half the country is on a diet of some kind and most
seven year old girls have had a riding lesson."

Oh god. I sensed another Mills moment. They clearly had
not experienced the hunger that I had during my week or the
terror as I got onto that horse, let alone the extraordinary
pain in my inner thighs the following morning from desperately trying to make it move.

"What do you suggest then?" I cleverly switched the onus
back to them.

"Ring up racehorse trainers," one fired back to a chorus of
approval, "get one who will take you on and teach you."

Maybe I hadn't been so clever.

Now, dear reader, I don't know how you feel about cold
calling busy and important people who are the heartbeat of

a thriving industry and asking them for help. But I didn't like the thought much. My Tiger was roaring!

Racehorse trainers may be a lot of things — entrepreneurs, salesmen and women, business people, employers, nurturers of talent, animal experts, logistics managers, race-readers and tacticians — but idiots they are not.

"Well, I do wish you luck Jim, and you're welcome to come and visit us, have a look about and grab a broom if you like, but it'd take a couple of years before I'd be comfortable putting you onto one of my horses. All the best!"

The Rulebook is being proved. I am meeting the guys on Friday. They'll expect better.

I ring around some of the racing bodies and schools in the UK and they are also very pessimistic. I am getting absolutely nowhere. I am not even eligible for consideration for the Foundation Course at the racing schools because I am over age. Nobody seems to know why the age limit is there. Nobody seems to want to question it either. This was a very interesting week for the Ten Rules and for the Tiger tamer himself. This was the week when I decided that I meant it. This was the week I discovered commitment.

I decided that it would happen. I had no idea how but it would happen. My first bold action would be to go on a real diet. My second bold action would be to buy a pair of running shoes (not since school had I worn sports shoes of any kind). My third would be to call Alcoholics Anonymous because I hadn't been to bed sober in over seventeen years. I didn't know anything about jockeys, but I couldn't imagine that this was recommended as a core part of the lifestyle and diet. This had to change and I had no idea how to conceive of a life without alcohol. I needed help there.

On the following Friday, I was eating salad with no dress-ing and drinking sparkling water — the guys were impressed. I was also leading a brainstorm on the boldest action that I could take. Some were looking a bit worried. I began to realise that some side bets were going on here and that me without a pint was a sign of something very serious going on, potentially even commitment!

We came up with a plan, my task for the following week: I was to ring up some of the most senior people in racing and ask them for assistance.

Now, dear Tiger tamer, I don't know how you feel about cold calling some of the most powerful and influential peo-ple in an industry. Personally, my Tiger was really getting to work as I started trying to make contact.

In the afternoon I started making my calls. Nothing has prepared me for the reaction that I receive. Everybody I call either takes the call or returns it promptly. Everybody is interested. Everybody wants to make it happen and offers some kind of help. One person I really want to speak with is Michael Caulfield, CEO of the Jockey's Association of Great Britain (now the Professional Jockeys Association). Surely he knows a thing or two about what is involved in being a jockey?

Only one problem: I have no number for him. So I email through their website and it is picked up by the leg-endary Ann Saunders MBE whom, at this point, I have never heard of. I had not even heard of Michael until the pre-vious Saturday's research, Ann passes the mail, asking Michael to call me, to the man himself. I know none of this until a number that I don't recognise flashes up on my mobile.

"Jim? It's Michael." From the conversations that followed, it became clear that I could win the bet if I really wanted to.

Within a couple of days I am having dinner with Michael and a woman I have never heard of called Gee Armytage. We are in a pub in a place I have never heard of called Lambourn. By the end of the evening, I am aware that Lambourn is one of the two major horseracing centres in England. These are just words at this time of night but soon I will see the bucking and kicking reality of strings and strings of racehorses — a sight that I still find as exciting now as I did the first time that I saw it.

And I have learned a little about the tiny and very beautiful Gee who radiates vitality across the table. It turns out that Gee Armytage is one of the first women to have ridden in the Grand National, the most famous race in the world and one of the most dangerous, the first to have ridden winners on level terms with men at Britain and Ireland's most cherished jumps meeting, the Cheltenham Festival. Now retired through injury, she remains one of the country's most successful and best known lady jockeys.

It turns out that Gee is engaged to be married to a man I have never heard of called Mark Bradburne, the jump jockey who was to come second in the Grand National on Lord Atterbury just a few months later and was to win the Ascot Chase on Hand Inn Hand in just a few weeks, and that she works as PA to one Anthony Peter McCoy MBE. At this point, I have not heard of AP McCoy either, but it turns out that he has ridden more winners than any other jump jockey in history. Gee asks a lot of questions and I try to answer them. I am sure to eat a salad and not to mention the word 'trifle'. Neither Michael nor Gee are heading for the dessert trolley either, and then Gee goes quiet, kind of thoughtful. So I keep quiet too.

"Okay then. If you are really up for it, I'll take you on. You need to be down here at 8am Saturday. I'll meet you in the car park of the Swan in Great Shefford, I'll get Candy Morris to open her shop early and we'll kit you out." I have not heard of Candy Morris. I'll introduce you to her later.

"Then we go to Martin Bosley's yard to watch them work the horses," Gee continues, "and then I'll try to get you a lesson with Tina Fletcher." You've guessed it, I've not heard of Martin or Tina either, but I should have, and I'll introduce them to you later too.

"What do you say?"

Oh no. Now I'm in trouble. Do I jump in the car fast and head for London? Or do I shake this woman's hand which she has extended across the dinner table, knowing that life will never be the same, and that it will probably be a lot less comfortable?

I say "yes". We shake hands. Michael smiles.

"Excellent. Gotta dash. See you Saturday. 8am." Gee Armytage is gone.

Michael and I chat on. He is about to leave the JAGB having just completed his studies to become a sports psychologist. He agrees to help also.

This is brilliant! The action has led to the commitment has led to two unbelievably talented coaches and supporters.

Game on.

*   *   *   *   *

There are many thrilling and wonderful experiences to be had in the world, but we do not need to seek thrills in the traditional, predictable way in order to get an adrenaline rush and experience life at full throttle. It could be that being genuinely radical and committed in one's approach to getting things done in the workplace could be just as thrilling, provide just as great an adrenaline hit, as a white water raft ride. Sometimes doing battle with the Tiger seems just one notch too high on the risk scale. People who are all up to try a charity skydive, or to dangle from ropes on a mountainside seem to falter and grind to a halt when facing a Tiger much closer to home.

We have looked together at why to act. We've looked at how it can lead to commitment, to the world giving us a bold result back, to support coming to us from the most surprising places, to getting the idea out there and started rather than having it fly around our head like a pinball being flipped back up in to the bells and lights every time it looks like escaping through the hole at the bottom of the table into a new place — into action and reality.

But what are the consequences of not acting? What are the consequences of staying comfortable and leaving the Tiger be?

The result of failing to take the bold action, of getting to grips with the Tiger, perhaps for the first time in any real sense, and beginning to write a different story is that you get to keep this one. Keep it safe, keep it stagnant, and, yes, this is as good as it gets. That may be fine, of course, But do take a moment to be sure of that before you decide. That day when we won't be able to write so fast is coming to us all.

Tomorrow

Ah, now here we meet the greatest lie of all: That tomorrow will be different. That tomorrow you will act boldly. That tomorrow, you will tame that Tiger. But you won't.

Tigers are not tamed tomorrow. Bold actions are not planned for tomorrow. It is all done today. It is all done now. It is a change in how we think, not a plan. And that's why Rule 1 is Rule 1 and not Rule 10. Because tomorrow feels just like today when it arrives, and one more day has passed with the Tiger writing the story. One more dent in our self-confidence.

Today is the only day that can count.

So how bold are you going to be? How are you going to discover that thrilling moment of absolute commitment, whatever the unlit and unknown road holds in store? Who knows what friends are there to be met along the way.

Rule 1: Act boldly today — time is limited.

Over to you.

Case study: Murray Elliot

Before I went to see Jim the year before last at a conference, I was a club archer. I had even represented Scotland a couple of times, but hadn't really pushed myself to take it that step further. For a few years I had been talking to people about the disabled Olympics, or Paralympic squad. People had suggested that with my physical disabilities, I might qualify, but I had never done anything much about it.

> "This time I wasn't going to drop it until I got somewhere. Within two or three months I was invited to a talent identification weekend where I was told that I was absolutely appropriate for the Paralympic squad."

There was a point in Jim's Taming Tigers presentation when he spoke about how limited time is and how, if you want to do something, you need to move towards it today, and also about making sure you stand on your own two feet and speak to the people you need to speak to in order to progress. I thought, "He's right." There were lots of things he said that tied together almost as a philosophy for life and it had a significant impact on me.

After the talk I took some steps and got in touch with people about the Paralympic squad. I had started this process before and had written applications only to not really follow them up, but this time I thought, "I'm actually going to do this, or I am always going to wonder about it." This time I wasn't going to drop it until I got somewhere.

Within two or three months I was invited to a talent identification weekend where I was told that I was absolutely appropriate for the Paralympic squad and, in fact, I would be one of the guys to challenge their existing athletes. I then contacted various people with the aim of finding appropriate coaching facilities and getting someone to coach me. I stuck my neck on the line a bit and told people what I was doing and through that I managed to get free training facilities. Following that, I was delighted to be offered a place on the Paralympic team development squad and I was invited to join the British Paralympic Association's fast track, which offers additional training with a view to getting to the Paralympics. This meant that I was looking at getting to London 2012, but I was also told that Beijing was an option. Going from being a club archer to imagining I might be in the running for Beijing was a huge leap!

Once I had heard that news, I did some more asking around and managed to get myself into the Eastern Scotland Institute for Sport, which helps athletes to receive additional training, including psychology, lifestyle and fitness. Before now, nobody had been doing these things for me but, thinking back to Jim's talk, I realised I needed to go and speak to the right people and drive this forward on my own behalf. The East of Scotland Institute for Sport offered me membership and gave me the additional training I needed for free which was extremely valuable. Unfortunately, in the end I wasn't able to go to Beijing because of administrative reasons beyond my control, but 2012 is getting closer every day.

Everything that happened has really turned my life inside out. I find I'm taking more charge of lots of things in my life as a result, such as work and financial commitments, because you have to make a plan to deliver yourself into a high performance environment. I've had to change my diet too.

The whole experience has brought about a fundamental change which has been scary but exciting too. The way I look at my sport and also the way I see my work life has really changed. The amount of time and effort I have put in to me as an individual has also increased but, fortunately, I've got a wife who is supportive; she is competitive in archery too so she understands what I'm trying to do, which is absolutely vital.

I went into Jim's speech with an open mind as I hadn't really seen any motivational speakers before. You hear about people going to see them and they come away talking about it and it all sounds great but nothing actually changes. I thought Jim's speech would be a bit of light entertainment in the middle of a long conference — I wasn't expecting to make any life changing decisions. Since then I've seen two other speakers. One was quite entertaining but didn't really tell me anything, and the other I found interesting but didn't take much away with me in terms things to apply to my life.

I think my main Tiger is my lack of self-confidence and self-belief. It's that little voice that keeps saying, "You're not good enough". There's a bit in Jim's speech where he talks about the guy going up to the beautiful woman to chat her up and the little voice is saying, "You're not good enough. Get back in your box." Since going through this process, my self-belief has expanded enormously. My friends and family were supportive, which is important, but even more so, people in the sport who didn't know me were giving me the affirmation that they thought I was good enough.

I've certainly had a few setbacks along the way. This year I've had a lot of coaching from people who didn't really know me, or understand me as a person, and as a result my performance has actually dipped in the last season. There have been times when I've felt that old Tiger coming back. At my first international event this year, my first time in the British team shirt, I shot so badly I burst into tears afterwards. I knew I was more than capable of beating the people on that field but I was shooting so badly. It was a really a massive downer for me after all the training but in the end I thought, "I can do this! I do want to get to London 2012 and whatever the issues, I'll cope and resolve them."

I'm now making a plan to recover technically and emotionally and get rid of the performance anxiety. In the end, even the difficulties have been a positive experience because I've learned a lot of valuable lessons about myself and the way I perform and, after all, they are just Tigers I need to tame.

Chapter 5

Rule 2: Re-write your Rulebook — challenge it hourly

So why was your guide to Tiger taming so slow to take a bold action to win his bet?

Because I had a Rulebook and I was acting according to it. My actions were being dictated by it.

My Rulebook, whatever my brave words to my challenger from the stage might have been, was that thirty-five year old, overweight, smoking, drinking business consultants who went to large state schools in densely populated, urban south London did not become jockeys. Little guys, probably aged around sixteen, who had been riding horses since they were six months old and who lived in the country, with family connections to racing — those were the people who became jockeys.

And you have a Rulebook too. How has it been guiding you for these past years? What is it stopping you from doing today? What has it stopped you becoming today? Will it stop you the same way tomorrow?

And the Rulebook is one of the most terrifying ways that the Tiger attacks us. Terrifying because the rules appear to be real, intellectually justifiable and often, in our minds, unchangeable. But this is all a fiction designed to keep us in the safety zone, designed to keep the Tiger on top. Let me explain.

We all have a Rulebook in our heads. It's how we see the world. In other places you will see this written as beliefs, but I don't think that that word is powerful enough. I don't think that that word begins to give us the full extent of what we're up against here. It's a rule because it often appears to us to be written in stone. It is a rule because often it has come to us from society, from our peers, from the culture of our workplaces — because if was we act against these rules without care, there may well be genuine consequences for us. This is no 'belief', this is a reality!

Except, of course, it isn't. It isn't real at all. It's just lots of people subscribing to the same rule. I am not speaking about the law of our land, about the rules of your religion, about our morals or our conscience. I'm not talking about the ways in which we have learnt to behave in order to do the right thing by our families and others around us.

I'm not talking about rules that can be proven. I am not talking about the fact that if we walk off the edge of a cliff, there will be a whistling sound in our ears before a long silence commences. I am talking about the kind of rule that says "I can't swim" or "I am great at maths but I can't write essays" or "this meeting will mock me if I put forward my idea."

We use these rules to make sense of the world. We use these rules to navigate. We use these rules to keep ourselves safe.

We create these rules to make ourselves safe.

And if we even consider disobeying them, the Tiger roars at us and we feel fear and insecurity. Let me give you an example. You are in a bar with some friends — whatever age you are, whatever gender you are — and you see a beautiful person on the other side of the bar. There they are in all their glory.

And you think to yourself, "Wow. Look at that beautiful person. I think I am going to have to go and speak to that beautiful person. Perhaps that beautiful person will speak back to me. Perhaps the beautiful person and I will become friends and who knows what will follow from that!"

I ought to point out that if you intend to practice this experiment, most people's Rulebook will dictate that you should be single when you do so.

So you begin to stroll across the bar towards your beautiful person with your thoughts full of witty lines and opening gambits, until you are just six strides away, when you catch, out of the corner of your eye, the toilet door. And as if by magic you find that you are, a moment later, in the toilet cursing yourself in the mirror rather than engaging your beautiful person in conversation.

What went wrong?

I believe it is the Rulebook that sabotages us and saves us from danger. So, as we walk over with our head full of wit, towards our beautiful person, the Rulebook begins to monkey around with us.

"I don't think you should do that," it warns.

"Why not?"

"Because that is a very beautiful person."

"I know. That's the whole idea here."

"But you are an ugly person!"

"That bad?"

"Have you looked in a mirror recently, my friend?"

"Do you think I could get away with using a bit of wit and charm?"

"Ha-ha-ha. For you, that was quite witty. I don't think so."

"I think she's seen me. I'm committed here, what should I do?"

"Look over her left shoulder. There's the loo. Go to the loo! Go to the loo!"

And somehow we end up visiting the toilet before reappearing at our original table and resuming our conversation with our friends. And isn't life grand! Instead of having to go through all the inconvenience of communicating with another human being, we have managed to fit in a trip to the toilet and plant ourselves back to enjoy a drink and some familiar conversation with our friends. And the failure of our mission wasn't even our responsibility. It was that beautiful person's fault! That person who judged us as too ugly to speak to them. That person who was so shallow and wouldn't give the time of day to somebody like us.

Of course, you have no idea what their reaction would have been. In fact, all you have done is follow your Rulebook, even reinforcing it to yourself in the process.

This rule is a fiction. We know it is not a real rule. We know this because in the world there are some incredibly ugly people going out with some fantastically beautiful ones.

They have all rewritten their Rulebook.

Of course, it is not impossible that they have also earned just a little bit of cash to help oil the wheels of life. But even at that — think about it for a moment — unless they sauntered up to the beautiful person and threw their Lamborghini keys down on the bar before they opened their mouth, they too have had to overcome that "whoops, batting above your average here, sunshine!" feeling as they wandered across the bar. They must have challenged the Rulebook.

How to spot your rules

Okay, here's something you can do straightaway to begin to examine how your rules are working to keep you safe from living your life. Either in your head or on a piece of paper, imagine a place that you would really like to get to. It doesn't matter whether that end place is to do with your work, friends, family, community, or sporting interests. Just write a place where you'd really like to get to — something that you'd like to achieve. Next, either write down or think through all of the reasons why you know that it's impossible for you to do that.

Now, carefully go through the reasons that you have written. Which of them are real reasons? Reasons that you can prove. Reasons that you have actually tested — that you could defend in a tough TV interview? Reasons that, if somebody offered you a vast sum of money (or whatever it is that turns you on) to overcome, you wouldn't be able to overcome in a flash!

Now you're beginning to discover the extent of your Rulebook — those cosy assumptions that are there to keep you safe.

Have a think about it. It could well be that a big bold
Rule 1 action coupled with a bit of Rule 5 (seeking tools for
Taming Tigers) could blast you straight past all of the rules
that you have just written down.

Corporate Rulebooks

Collectively, we love these rules. Collectively, we create
them with wild enthusiasm, because, collectively, as individ-
ually, we crave to know how it works. We desperately want
to be able to predict the outcome. To get it right, just like we
were taught we could in the classroom to. But we can't get it
right like that in the real world. There is rarely a right
answer, just the best answer that we can come up with. And
if that answer is to be a progression from the previous model,
we need to break some of the rules that we used to build the
earlier one! The more predictable we manage to make it, the
more predictable we make the irrelevance of our organisation over a matter of time.

What is the difference in the approach to the corporate /
cultural Rulebook that enables one company to say, "Hmm.
We sell computers in an increasingly competitive environment and our market share is being squeezed. I think we
should invest in some extremely expensive salespeople,
equip them with expensive cars and executive airline loyalty
cards and send them out into the world to regain market
share for us."

Or, "Hmm. We sell computers in an increasingly competitive environment and our market share is being
squeezed. We think we should shift all of our manu-
facturing to the East, where we can reduce costs, increase

margin and decrease price to the consumer all at the same time!"

When a third company is thinking, "Hmm. We sell computers in an increasingly competitive environment and our market share is being squeezed. What we need to do is diversify out of this market. How can we leverage our brand loyalty most out there? Oh, yeah. I know! Let's invent a really funky MP3 player and hook it up to an online music store. And if that works, we'll use all of our technical abilities to create the funkiest phone in town."

I'm not going to pass any kind of judgement on the strategies deployed above, I'll leave that to the experts. What fascinates me is the ability within some organisations for people like you and me to take decisions and create actions that are creative, dynamic and are backed by passion and pace, whereas others make their old mistakes, just in a slightly more desperate way.

How many Tigers must there be roaring when you take the decision to break the proven and acknowledged rule that says, "search engines are made up of a busy, cluttered interface full of banner ads and links to other pages which will try to exploit different revenue earning opportunities with a small box on the front allowing people to search the Internet"? How many Tigers must have been roaring when they thought, "I will invest everything I own to create a clear white space with a box in the middle and a funky logo. My revenue model shall be to bring small, affordable, non-design led 'banner ads' to the attention of the searcher at the point in which they are proactively interested in finding information on that subject matter! Oh, and by the way, did I tell you that I'm going to create a bidding market for those advertisements based on near-perfect information as to the demand and supply of that information within the market?"?

There would be Tigers around as you pitched those ideas. And yet they have changed our world and made people very rich. Some companies can re-create their Rulebooks — and know how to forget old useless rules quickly. Some companies embed Tiger Taming.

Conventional wisdom

We are surrounded by conventional wisdom. And we follow it. Being conventional is a very safe thing to be, after all. It keeps you with the majority and staying there minimises exposure and risk. But how did all that conventional wisdom get there? Did conventional people put it there? Do conventional people like to rise above the warm sludge of mediocrity to write their stories? Are conventional people obsessed with running safely and securely with the pack, especially on such tricky matters as wisdom, where we would not want to be judged and seen to be wanting?

Conventional wisdom is the Tiger tamer's biggest enemy. It is the collective Tiger at work. Following conventional wisdom will give us conventional results in our chosen sphere of operations. And your boredom with conventional results is, I hope, why you have read this far in this book. And does that mean you should question the Rules for Taming Tigers also? You betcha. Believe nothing I say. What on Earth do I know? But if our relationship through these pages causes you to start asking those questions, then let us both consider this process a great success, shall we?

The fear of failure

And what is it the rules do so brilliantly for us? They keep us safe. But safe from what? Safe from the possibility of failure. And one of the rules that we were taught so carefully at such a young age ("Name me The Six Wives of King Henry VIII!" — my hand remained firmly down, and I tried to avoid the teacher's gaze. Yours?) is the fear of failure. The "but what if ...?" And at this stage it is traditional to say that we should not fear failure. That failure is an acceptable part of reaching our successes. What unconscionable tripe and unhelpful insanity. At this stage I am, traditionally, supposed to tell you about how many filaments Edison burned before he managed to get one that would exist within the vacuum that we refer to as a light bulb, and how this never perturbed him. I never had the honour of meeting Mr Edison, but I bet it got right up his nose. I bet he feared failure. I bet Mrs Edison feared it quite a lot too. I bet it made him work really hard. I wonder if his utter horror of the idea of failing *at what he had committed heart and soul to achieve* drove him to many sleepless nights.

But we also know that something also drove him to work and think and work and think and question until he achieved greatness. Perhaps that something was a fear of not getting there – a fear that he would fail.

Do entrepreneurs who have burned all financial bridges, and thrown their heart and soul into a project, wake up in the middle of the night driven by thoughts of attaining great wealth or by thoughts of avoiding great poverty? Which is the driver? Fear of failure.

So, contrary to conventional wisdom, let's fear failure. Let's take *not* failing really seriously. Recognise that fear for the lousy Tiger that it is and use these rules to counteract the effect of the fear as it works on you, but never allow that fear to paralyse you. Never allow the fear to re-write the story that is rightfully yours. The fear of mounting a horse on Wednesday that bolted with you terrifyingly on Monday, that fired you into the ground at high speed on Tuesday, is real. But every work rider in racing and, for sure, every jockey has taken the decision to mount the horse and try for the third hair-raising time. They all fear failure and for pretty good reason. And for some, certainly, that fear will drive them to choose not to mount the horse on Wednesday. They will either accept that they have reached their limits and cannot progress further onto such tricky beasts, or they will leave this occupation and move onto another, only to find a limitation there that will drive them on to another again. They have allowed the Tiger to write their story, to divert them from their sense of purpose. Pain is temporary, but failure lasts forever, as they say.

The origins of the Rulebook

So where do these rules come from? These rules that we cling to keep us safe and that we are so slow to question, challenge and change. Well, of course, they come from all sorts of influences.

I don't know where your rules come from, of course. I have no idea how easy or tough the journey has been and what you have learned along the way. I know some of mine and I'll now highlight some that we are likely to share. But before I do, here's a question to you, Tiger tamer: are you the kind of person who's going to construct and live by a personal navigational system based on "all sorts" of different unquestioned influences? Is that good enough for you or will you have to experiment, take risks and continually challenge your Rulebook? Perhaps hourly?

1 *Family*

The most common answer when I ask an audience where our Rulebook comes from. But do we really want to write a Rulebook based on the way our parents acted and spoke in order to keep us safe when we were nine years of age? Did they send you off to school with a cheery "Goodbye, dear. Have a great day! Be sure to take risks today! Make your mark out there today. Shake 'em up a bit!"? No, probably quite the opposite and, of course, while that was a good rule for a nine year old child, stopping them from having a really tough time at school, it might impede the progress of a twenty-nine year old who's trying to make an impact on their world.

2 *Other people's rules about you*

What are other people's rules about you?
Now this is different, of course, for everybody. But it's very interesting to watch.

As they reflect their personal assumptions about your limitations back at you, are you paying attention to what they're saying and internalising it? Or are you listening to what they say with the ability to critically challenge it in your mind?

Apart from my mother, there were only three people initially who didn't laugh at either their friend "Jim Lawless" or, if they didn't know me, "that bloke of thirty-five who wants to race", who took it in their stride: Michael Caulfield, Gee Armytage and my daughter, Maddie. Some family members were quite derisory. Many people smiled and saved their sarcasm for a later conversation with somebody else. These people will, of course, impact on and assist you in forming your own Rulebook, but that is all they should be doing, assisting.

You hold the pen.

3 Our experiences

And then there are our experiences. And, let's face it, we're not stupid, are we? We don't make the same mistake twice, do we? We like to learn our limitations. Only a fool would step beyond their limitations, overstep their own personal mark. Isn't that right?

Well, let's just think this through in action. Let's take the scary world of a presentation. You give one. It goes badly. How do you know it went very badly? Because you get feedback to tell you that it went very badly.

And now, of course, it is the twenty-first century and we have 360 degree feedback. This means that everybody is now entitled to tell you that it went very badly!

So you go home bruised and slightly battered. And we soon learn where our limitations lie, don't we? And surely only a fool would work outside or beyond their limitations? And so we write a new rule into the Rulebook, "I am not a good presenter. I do not do presentations. They cannot make me. But if they do make me, then I will stand at the side of the room talking at my laptop and screen rather than engaging with the audience."

Of course, this is just one approach. A perfectly reasonable alternative is to decide that you are never going to make the mistake of performing a skilled task in front of an audience without training and preparing yourself for it first. So you take a course, you rehearse in front of your peers, you get the skill perfected and then you deliver presentations well. But it is our choice. We can construct a rule to keep us safe from this dangerous area and it can begin to become our reality.

But imagine if our children obeyed their Rulebooks. Imagine if a child learning to walk did as an adult might do and decided that, seeing as they are clearly no good at walking (they know this because the entire living room has been laughing at their attempts and their tumbles for the last three to six months), they will settle for the toddler's equivalent of staring at the laptop at the side of the presentation room. They decide that, as walking is clearly beyond them, they'll stick to crawling. And there they stay.

As children or as adults the ability to question and redefine our Rulebooks dictates the speed at which we learn, develop and progress. For those who dislike challenging this Rulebook intensely the result is, of course, utter stagnation — often coupled with embitterment and a victim mentality.

A 'victim mentality'? Sure. "It's not my fault it's the rules — be they the rules left me by my family, my hardships in life, my controlling boss, my partner, my genes or my experiences. It's not a Tiger. It's not a lack of guts. It's 'them'. Experience has taught that it is 'them'." And no evidence of others moving onwards and upwards in their lives will convince them to admit to what they know in their hearts. They're staying safe with the cosy rules!

Let's look at this another way. A few years ago, I helped my daughter learn to ride a bicycle without stabilisers. I had

kind of pushed her into making this step. She wasn't all
that keen, but she was beginning to become frustrated at
the fact that many of her friends could ride a two-wheeler,
while it was something she had yet to get to grips with.
So, the fateful Saturday arrived and I ran around bent
double, with my hand underneath the saddle for an hour or
so before she peddled off away from me. I stood up straight
again and enjoyed the view: This little girl, with her funny
hat on, hair blowing out behind her, wobbling her way down
the path.

After a couple of seconds, I could almost sense her realising that she was no longer being supported by me. She knew
that I couldn't run that fast! She turned to see how far she
had come, and gave me a smile which soon turned to shock
before she turned her head straight again, wobbled horribly
and met the path with a crunch.

By the time I reached Maddie, there were tears and
there was blood. She looked at me with amazement in
her eyes that I had pushed her into something that caused
her to be lying in a crumpled heap on the ground. And I
felt dreadful that I was responsible for abusing my child
in this way. So we took the bicycle back home, we put
the stabilisers back on, and Maddie has ridden happily
on her four-wheeled bike ever since. I don't care if Maddie
turns out to be the only thirty-nine year old woman
riding around London with stabilisers on her bicycle;
I am not going to damage my child on her precious week-
ends!

Well, of course, I didn't do that. We abandoned the bicycle and we went over to the swings in the park, and after
thirty minutes of playing and eating ice cream, we gave it

another try, and within an hour she raced me back to our front door, and won by a country mile.

So here's my question to you: When experience teaches you that something can go wrong, and that when it does it will hurt you in a real, grown up way, who helps you to pick yourself up? Who helps you to get back on to the bicycle once you've cleared off the blood and try again? Who helps you to avoid constructing a nice rule to keep yourself safe from ever having to take that risk again?

Somebody may help you. It is very exciting if somebody does. It is also rare. Even those who love us often want us to avoid pain — they may well rather we didn't get "back on the bike". They may fear that if we are on the bike, then they are under pressure to be also — and that may not sit well with them. The harsh reality may be that it is down to us to do battle with the Tiger and refuse to be beaten into writing a rule that keeps us safe from writing our story.

Re-writing the Rulebook — the real secret to increasing confidence

There are hokum CDs that you can buy tucked away inside hokum books that will promise to deliver you extra confidence while you sleep or while you read. But where does confidence come from? Why do great jockeys look so confident on horses that are bucking and kicking beneath them, whereas most mortals look nervous on a horse that is plodding gently along a country lane?

I'll give you a clue: They didn't get it from a CD or a book.

They got that confidence from sitting on a lot of horses. They got it from pushing their boundaries and sitting on more difficult horses. They got it knocked when those more difficult horses threw them on the ground in a crumpled mess as they stretched beyond their current limitations in a bid to become better and better. And then they built it again when they eventually battled with themselves until they could ride that horse and then it was time to move to a more difficult horse again.

They got it because they challenged their Rulebook, a Rulebook that would have said that they had found their limitations, but that they refused to accept.

It's my belief that the real secret to building confidence lies in challenging our Rulebook, in creating a new Rulebook along the lines of the model that you can see in Chapter 10. And as soon as you begin to feel comfortable with your new Rulebook, challenging it and developing again. And confidence is also built by working on the Esteem Rule, Rule 10, 'Never, never give up'. But more of that to come.

For now, let's go back to that exercise at the beginning of the chapter. Let's look even more closely and critically at the rules that would stop you acting to write the next chapter of your story as you would wish it written. Let's look at the Tiger at work there.

How much time must pass before you strike the Tiger's rules out and replace them with the ones you wish or even need to see there? What are the opportunities passing by in the interim?

Over to you.

Case study: Peter Winters

I had worked in pharmaceutical market research for fifteen years. In the last few years I had started to think increasingly about the challenge of climate change and in my spare time I started reading up on it and thinking, "What can we do about it?" I thought about what I could do but was struggling to see a commercial opportunity in that area.

"It makes you challenge yourself and say, "Are you brave?" Part of my business plan was to sell my house in the UK which was a risk, but it was worthwhile in order to be able to start the business."

I attended a talk by Jim Lawless in Malta last year. I had no real preconceptions when going to see him but I heard that he had a good reception with the same group at the previous event and thought, as it had been recommended, it might be worth going along. I found Jim's talk both entertaining and motivating — he makes you feel like you can do anything — and I took a leaflet home afterwards. What struck me about Jim is that he had the balls to take up a challenge himself. Something he said that really hit home for me was that nobody wanted to be old and sitting in a nursing home reminiscing and feeling like they'd missed their chance. It's a powerful idea.

I started thinking again about what I might be able to do with climate change. I spoke to someone else who had attended the talk afterwards. She had come especially to see Jim's talk and she was very encouraging too. I said to her, "I do have this idea and I need to do something about it." It was a combination of Jim's talk and speaking to her that got me started.

A couple of things then happened in my personal life. My wife is French Canadian, and had decided she wanted to move back to Montreal. That was the trigger to take the plunge, give up pharmaceuticals and see what I could do with climate change. I came up with the idea of setting up a research agency, carrying out a syndicated survey on the market and climate change, and then selling the data.

The challenge for me was the leap into the unknown. The first step was moving to Canada as it gave me the opportunity to make a change. I had to leave my job but I had some savings, and as Canada is a lower-cost environment than the UK, there were good conditions for setting up a business.

I put together a plan looking in detail at the challenges of climate change. I did a lot of research and then put together a fifty-one page document containing a plan to help clients understand what's going on with climate change. I think it's important to be pointing in the right direction and know where you're going. Without having a plan, I think you can lose direction. I started sending it out and got a lot of nice comments on it, lots of people were interested in the document and in potentially buying the data. Three or four people who read it said they wanted to work with me and I was able to form a management team of four or five people.

Jim is very can-do and brave. That's what comes through more than anything else. It makes you challenge yourself and say, "Are you brave?" Part of my business plan was to sell my house in the UK which with the state of the housing market was a risk, but it was worthwhile in order to be able to start the business.

I think trying to do something scary every day is a good motto. Sometimes I do, sometimes I don't. But I think that that once you have committed yourself to doing something, you have to do it and you'd look a fool if you didn't. The situation you put yourself in when you commit to something makes things scary every day anyway.

Work does get wrapped up in my personal life. I'm married with two small children and moving to Canada, finding a new house, all took a lot of time. There's a bit of juggling going on but if I still worked for a big company, I wouldn't have the freedom to do that.

I haven't hit any obstacles that made me want to give up but I find you have to be alert for potential problems in the future. Yesterday, someone who was going to do something quite important for the business realised that it wasn't going to work for him. It could have been a problem but I had a back up arrangement. You don't always know what's going to work in business planning, so it's always a good idea to have an alternative plan.

Overall, the project has worked really well so far and I have had lots of support from people who would like to join the team. More than I anticipated, in fact. The first report will launch on 22nd October 2008 and we will see where we go after that.

Chapter 6

Rule 3: Head in the direction of where you want to arrive, every day

When the Ten Rules were first put together and used in industry, I was foolish enough to think that I had them cracked. That was a big error of judgment.

I am learning faster about them today than I did even during my racing year or when I was using them in change programmes. This is partly because I try to continue to play for interesting stakes personally, which always produces a healthy roar from my Tiger, and partly because, at the time of writing, over seventy thousand people around the world have heard a Taming Tigers presentation or attended a workshop, and they often get in contact. They'll tell me things about the Rules and how they have experimented with them or have attached a different meaning to a Rule than I had been thinking about.

One Rule that I learned a great deal about during my riding adventure was Rule 3, 'Head in the direction of where you want to arrive, every day'. I learned more about it

largely through being fortunate enough to be close to professional sportspeople in the racing world, and by that phrase I
mean both trainers and jockeys. Originally, Rule 3 was
about goal-setting and creating a plan. Simple. But I don't
think I had really seen how seriously this can be taken, or the
power of the results that can be achieved, until I got an inside
look at the world of sport. The power of Rule 3 then became
apparent, along with the degree of Tiger taming involved to
really use it to its full extent.

Rule 3 as taught by professional sportspeople

Now I don't know what it is like where you work, but when
I was office-based, I worked in places where the routine was
to arrive in the morning with a nice cup of takeaway coffee
and congregate with others to have a chat about people who
had not yet arrived. Then some folk would move off to their
desks and others would arrive. Then the conversation would
shift to those people who had just left the group. And finally,
the time would come to go and see what the great and mer-
ciless god "Outlook" had sent us to do that day. Not every
day would start this way, but it was not a rarity.

Sport is different — your results count. Or rather, *only*
your results count — the fact that you attended does not.
Results are not available every day, so you plan hard to
achieve them. It is thrilling to watch and to take part in. An
athlete knows the date of a big day far in advance, so the
plan works back from that day. And it covers everything:
nutrition, mental wellbeing, sleep, fitness, strength, tactics,
observing the competition and their likely approach, and
finally, rehearsing the skill that they will perform — from a

tennis swing to riding a horse at speed over five foot high fences.

But what is your big day?

What result are you working towards? What is the point of it all? What is the climax of this chapter of your story and what is the chapter you're thinking of writing next? Now hold on before you get too testy with me. Yes, I know I'm prodding, but why are you so sensitive to the prod? And no, it's not different just because you work in a regular job or [insert another excuse that you like, personally], that is merely a rule from you Rulebook.

Yes, I know that you probably don't want to be a sportsperson and that you may think that there is little that you can learn from their unhealthy levels of obsession — and especially from jockeys for heaven's sake! But I'm not talking about big macho 'goals' here (unless that's your personal bag), I'm simply talking about the thing that you are working towards.

To keep you from deciding that this chapter is not important to you, consider this:

1. **The place you want to arrive at needn't be 'traditional'.**

   The position that you are working daily to arrive at can range from some fabulous public achievement or the gaining of material wealth to the creation of a new habit that means that "I make people smile when I meet them" or "I decline all meetings that are a waste of my time." Both are worthwhile climaxes to any chapter in your story, and both involve taming a Tiger and changing your world and your story for the better when you start to do them.

2. Somebody is writing the story that is unfolding.

Your story to date is made up of the sum of your choices, your decisions to act or refrain from acting. Either the pen is writing with purpose or it is doodling. If it is doodling, there is no need to face a Tiger at any stage. Why would you battle with it for no reason? That means that the Tiger is writing your story. It must be. We don't battle with the Tiger without a motivation to do so. Good luck when we meet in the nursing home, matey — this'll be one for the grandchildren!

3. I know that you don't have time.

Nobody does. That is the single most common response to an introduction to Tiger taming. I have had whole rooms filled with sales people who aren't hitting their numbers call out almost as one that "they don't have time" when it comes to creating the plan, and acting on it, in order to rectify the disaster that they are so 'busy' creating. Please read Rules 2, 8 and 1, in that order, if you truly believe that you "don't have time". If you don't truly believe it, throw away the crutch!

Now, let's go back to where we were for a moment and look again at what there is to be learned from the sportspeople.

So, an athlete knows the date of a big day far in advance. And the date of the big day doesn't change, you're either ready or you're not. And if you are not, you lose. And you don't buy the new car. Perhaps you don't even get to pay the rent. The result counts.

And this is the world in which I began to discover what Rule 3 really meant. And this is where you and I are going to go now to explore the enormous power of deadlines, committed plans and, most importantly, of reaching clarity about where it is that you are headed. Because we are all headed somewhere, whether we have reached clarity about it and have a plan to create it or not.

A sense of purpose — nectar to the human soul

If there is one effect that delivering the Taming Tigers speeches and seminars around the world seems to have had more than anything else, it is to assist people in creating, discovering or rediscovering a sense of purpose. The Rules have done the same for me over the past five years. By identifying the Tiger and how to tame it, they can see themselves as free to get on with writing the story that they want to write for themselves, their family, their colleagues and their communities. They develop a strong desire to get on with the next thing, and they see that it is possible. They start to see success as a possible outcome and that's an encouraging place to get to.

You have met people with a sense of purpose. Maybe you have been such a person. Maybe you are today. You know the glow that radiates off of a person who has purpose. You have seen the optimism in their eyes. You have wondered at their ability to make clear decisions based on some solid core. And you may have thought them 'brave' because they are willing to deal with Tigers to move forward. You have probably referred to them as 'inspirational' or 'a breath of fresh air'.

These 'inspirational' people come in all shapes and sizes. The sixty-five year old who suddenly decides to face their fears and learn to drive in order to play an active part in the lives of their grandchildren. The unassuming person who has quietly dedicated four decades to spreading a passion for novels in the local school. The man who goes into a prison in 1964 stating a willingness to die for the cause of a "democratic and free society in which all persons live together in harmony" and repeats that same intention immediately as he emerges into the world in 1990.

They all have a sense of purpose and we remember them for it, we love them for it. They inspire us. They change us and they change our worlds.

A sense of purpose gives our lives meaning and gives each dawn a meaning. It drives our decisions and gives us a reason to be courageous and tenacious when the moment suddenly and unexpectedly challenges us. Acting in accordance with our sense of purpose gives us the last plank in the Integrity Rules.

And so you see that this chapter need not be about a lofty Olympian dream or some greed-fuelled desire for financial advancement (although it can be, for sure). It can simply be to make more people laugh; to teach your children well in that tiny window of time that you have to influence them, rather than leave them to the mercies of the people who pay for their TV programmes; to help the people who look to us daily to lead them to see their possibilities and to leave them standing taller not smaller at the end of each day.

If you're a jockey, of course, it may be to win the Grand National, one of the most famous and expensive races on planet Earth. And that date is not going to change. You need to be ready.

Athletes and Rule 3

On Grand National Day, a piece of history will be made. The events of the race and the result will be remembered and talked about in thirty years' time and beyond. Get ready or miss your place in the history books. Simple.

And I think that that is why they don't seem to start their days very often with a takeaway coffee and a conversation about their colleagues. They don't ever start their work with a review of demands made upon them through their email inbox. They wake with a driving purpose for what must be achieved that day.

A driving purpose for what must be achieved that day if they are to arrive in the right state when the big day arrives; if they are to write the story that they want to write for themselves. They have a plan to achieve that and they need to execute on that plan. They need to take the step today or there will be too many steps to cope with tomorrow. Today counts.

Now an athlete is not as different from you and me as you might suspect. They do have emails, and phones, and numerous demands on their time. They have relationships to nurture and children to care for and socks to be washed ready for the week ahead and cars to get serviced and food to be bought. Unlike most of us, they also have charity demands placed upon them very frequently and if they are too busy to spend time with journalists they will often find that this can lead to unfortunate consequences for them. Jockeys also have riding boots that need a daily polish.

But if they don't balance those obligations with moving forward towards the place where they want to be, they will fail to arrive there. So where they do tend to differ from many of us is that:

- they have a clear sense of where they need to get to;
- they have a clear plan to get to that place;
- they are committed to following that plan;
- they face Tigers if necessary in order to prioritise that plan rather than the other stuff.

If you meet an athlete at the end of a day when he or she has failed to move forwards, when they failed to achieve what needed to be achieved today, when something went wrong, they are very, very bad company. Why? Because it mattered and because it will be tough, if not impossible, to put it right tomorrow. Tomorrow has its own tasks. A day has been lost. The prize became just a little less certain.

Everything achieved has first been imagined

Now think for a moment about something that you have done — anything from passing a tricky exam to riding a horse to making the garden look nice.

You imagined it first.

You may not have sat down in a darkened room with some soothing music and painted yourself in your mind's eye receiving the exam result, or sitting on your horse, or in your nice garden, but you created the possibility that you could pass the exam, or ride the horse or improve the garden. It did not exist, yet you thought it a possibility.

Therefore, you imagined it.

Let's leave the jockeys for a moment. Think of an architect. Now when architects work, they go to a whole other level of imagining. They have clients who need to understand, planners who need to approve. It is their responsibility to improve that understanding and gain the approval, so they bring their imagination into two-dimensional reality by drawing what is in their mind. It existed first in their imagination. Then it was a drawing of something that they imagined. And then, one day, we saw it and gasped.

As soon as a child thinks about winning the Grand National, he or she has imagined it. When you speak to jump jockeys who have won the Grand National, the most intimidating and most famous jumps race on the planet, and ask what it meant to them, they will often reply that it fulfilled a childhood dream. When you ask when the dream started, they will all be very specific. He will start to go all dreamy and stare into the middle distance (a very unusual state to see a jump jockey in) and he will start talking about how it was a big annual tradition to watch the big race. He will start to talk about how he remembers the sound and the atmosphere coming through the TV screen. He will start to talk about how he imagined the crowd roaring as he cleared a two foot fence on a pony later that day.

He will describe how he began to dare to imagine the possibility of winning the Grand National. He will talk about how he began to watch his diet and keep himself fit and concentrate harder on his riding. He will describe how he used Rule 3 even before he had heard about it, because it isn't a rule that I created. It is a universal rule that has guided billions of people throughout time.

For some, as they start to grow up, those imaginings became goals that they were desperate to realize. And for some, they become a reality. The 'childhood dream', the imagined possibility became a reality because they, personally, made it their business to bring it to life. And for one, Mick Fitzgerald, the Irish jockey who won the Grand National in 1996 en route to becoming the fifth most successful jump jockey in history, that realization of a childhood dream was, in his words to the interviewer after the race, "better than sex".

We should not underestimate the importance of imagination, nor the ease with which our imagination can be squashed as we are told by others to 'get real', or as we face up to the challenge ourselves and start to 'get real' about the size of the task.

Many children don't get exposed to the thing that they may excel at. It is neither on the curriculum, nor on the television so they miss out. Who knows? You and I may be the greatest aeronautical engineers on the planet, it's just that at our schools they had only heard of doctors, accountants and lawyers! We need to imagine.

Now certain groups have pinched ideas such as imagination and have given them new names in order to claim these concepts for their own wide basket of borrowed and renamed ideas. But let's be really clear what we are talking about here. This is not a clever trick to reprogram your mind. This is, quite simply, permitting ideas to come into your head about what you want to do with your life. You don't need a course (or even this book) to help with that — it was alive as a way of making plans for your future long, long before the ancient Greeks imagined and created a democracy!

The Tiger attack

In a few pages, we will look at how Rule 3 can be used in practice. But first, I want to stress how important this Rule is in defending against the Tiger.

Rule 3 defends against the Tiger in three important ways:

1 **Rule 3 stops the Tiger from squashing your imagination.**

If you imagine a worthwhile thing, something that excites you, it is possible that it will seem impossible to achieve. If you imagine a worthwhile thing and you doodle on the back of an envelope what the first step might be to getting there, and the second, and the third, then it may just begin to become a possibility, especially if you have worked with Rule 2 effectively. Before you "get real" about your limitations — Rule 3 asks you to have a bash at building a plan. How does it look? Is it worth a little Rule 1 or Rule 5 work?

2 **Rule 3 requires you to decide on a place that you want to arrive at.**

Once you open that can of worms that is your imagination and start seeing possibilities through those doodles, who knows what place you may decide to strike out for, but one thing is likely, you will *want* to strike out to somewhere, despite the Tiger. You'll *want* to start writing the next chapter, despite the Tiger. You will *want* to have an exciting sense of purpose. So even before the Rule requires you to decide on a place, you will probably have done so of your own accord. But the Rule does require it. You cannot create a plan to get to a place that you have not yet imagined. So get imagining.

3 **Rule 3 requires you to create a plan to get to that place.**

Once you have a plan, you know what you are doing today. And once you know that, like the sportsperson, you can discriminate and prioritise. Now you have a reason to face up to your Tiger when a senior person or a client makes a request that would stop you arriving at your required resting point this evening.

Gee used Rule 3 (without knowing it — she's an athlete so I guess it was habit) to help me to believe that the project was possible. She used it to build my confidence. She used it to keep my imagination functioning.

"Leave the racing part to me," I was instructed, "All you have to do is what I ask you to do this week."

That sounded simple enough, but then I hadn't yet heard what she had in mind for the week. At that stage, I didn't believe that I would race. Not really. If I am honest, I could almost imagine it, but not enough to take it seriously. But Gee really did believe I would get to race. By requiring me to focus on that week's part of the plan, and to do that to the best of my ability, we were both dealing with my problem: that the end point was so unreal, I could not really imagine it.

Rule 3 and the plan to get to the racecourse

I believe that luck can sometimes play a part in life, but I'm not going to credit it for the fact that I had Michael Caulfield and Gee Armytage to work with me on creating a plan to get to the racetrack. I'm going to give all of that credit to Rule 1 of the Ten Rules for Taming Tigers. Maybe it was lucky that I caught them in a receptive mood when I made those calls, but they could have been in the best mood in the world and, had Rule 1 not made me pick up the phone and speak to these people, I would never have met them. Working with Gee and Michael meant that I could put in place a plan that I could cope with.

Let me explain that. As I mentioned when we looked at Rule 2 together, I had some pretty clear rules about jockeys. For all my bravado in accepting the bet, my real rules about jockeys were that they were very light, very talented on a horse, had probably been riding horses since they were three months old, were very brave and sporty, and knew lots of people in the racing community. The fact that I could tick not one of these boxes gave me cause for a lot of concern when I really began to look at the project. And that is where Rule 3 began to work its magic.

Gee and Michael were able to break down the tasks involved. Why? Because they knew what they were and I did not! Now Michael is a good horseman and worked in racing for many years, but he let Gee take the lead when it came to working on riding, diet and exercise. What else could there be, you might ask? Well, there were a variety of things that I hadn't even realised were going to make the plan a failure from day one unless they were addressed. Not least amongst these was that I needed to pay the mortgage and all my other outgoings, and was about to introduce a huge new activity into my working week. Secondly, I lived near Cobham at the time, south of London. The drive to Lambourn for a 6am start would prove quite difficult. I didn't mind the early mornings, but I was soon to discover that from 2pm each day I was well below par.

The wonderful thing about having a sense of purpose, which I think I'd first achieved when I shook hands with Gee in the Hare & Hounds that night, is that once the steps have been decided you can act decisively to make them happen. So I remember very clearly sitting in Michael Caulfield's cottage near Lambourn, working through the practical steps that I would need to take immediately if this project was to have any chance of success. The first was to move to Lambourn. The second was to transform how I organised my work into an extremely streamlined process.

When I'm speaking on stage, I don't have time to add in all these little details and still achieve the brief that the organisation has given me to achieve, so it's always frustrating to be talking to people afterwards and realise that they've gained the impression that I took a year's sabbatical to do this and that therefore, of course, life is different for them as they would not be able to take time off. They have to go to work every day so how can they possibly make a change in their lives? I want to add in here, so that anybody feeling daunted by the idea of juggling time can gain some encouragement: it can be done alongside the day job! Whether what you are trying to do is to work *within* your job to create change (which always has to be done alongside the daily grind) or whether you are doing something outside of the workplace, it can be done. Have a look at this chapter and at Chapter 11 looking at Rule 8. These are the important ones to read if you have any concerns about creating the time to make things different. Then go back and check out Rules 2 and 1, in that order.

Now as you will discover in Rule 5, 'The tools for Taming Tigers are all around you'. So as I looked blankly at Michael and asked if he knew any decent estate agents who might be able to rent me some very small and very reasonably priced accommodation in Lambourn, he sat back, took a swig from his coffee cup and, after a thirty second pause, said, "Let me give Charles and Merrigan a call."

I left my planning session with Michael with steps agreed regarding living and working in a way that would permit me to get to the racecourse in a year. It was a vital, vital meeting. As I mentioned previously, Michael was moving on from his post as Chief Executive of the Jockeys' Association of Great Britain (now the Professional Jockeys Association) and has established himself over the past five years as one of the leading sports psychologists in the UK working with county cricket teams, premiership football clubs and top golfers and jockeys. He brought this talent to bear on our conversation in highlighting to me the seemingly insignificant things that would overwhelm me and kill the project faster than any fall from a horse would do if I didn't get them straight and get them straight fast.

Meanwhile, you remember that dinner with Gee where she offered to take me to visit Candy Morris, Martin Bosley and Tina Fletcher?

Now Gee had to leave the pub shortly after we'd made this initial plan, to get home, and Michael and I had a coffee.

"Who's Tina Fletcher?" I asked.

"Who's Tina Fletcher?" asked Michael in amazement, "I keep forgetting that you really don't know anything about this world. Tina is one of the few hand-picked Olympic qualified equestrian coaches in the country. She's a champion show-jumper and she's married to Graham Fletcher who rode for Team GB in the Olympics and they've both ridden all over the world."

"Oh!"

Now in case you're wondering, no, I probably couldn't afford the fees for an Olympic equestrian coach. And, you're right, Olympic equestrian coaches don't really want to spend time with some novice from London, teaching them how to hold their hands on the reins. They tend to be more excited by working with Olympic-type people. The only reason I've got even a slim chance of working with someone of Tina's calibre is because Rule 1 has introduced me to Gee and Michael, and Rule 5 (The tools for Taming Tigers are all around you) is busy proving itself as Gee puts in a phone call to her friend the next morning and explains that she's just met some character from London who reckons he wants to ride on the racetrack — would she like to take a look?

I think that Tina accepted out of curiosity. I think she thought that it would be fun to watch this, if nothing else, and I think she also caught a little of Gee's enthusiasm for the mad project.

And now, before she's even met me, Tina is almost on the team!

But look what's happened. Look how the plan is reducing my battle with the (accurate) Rulebook that I have about my chances of success here. Suddenly I don't have to worry about that. Gee, Michael and Tina are experts and they think it's worth a shot. And *they* have dictated what my first steps should be.

So my plan in those early days is:

1. Chat to Merrigan and Charles Norwood about their tiny cottage that may be to let

Within two weeks I had let my property in London and moved into the cottage. Charles and Merrigan made me very welcome in a strange new land and I will always be grateful to them for that.

2. Create a plan to streamline my work to create more time

This plan is still in place today and has profoundly affected how I run my business. I used to spend around thirty-five percent of my time travelling to or sitting in sales meetings which yielded no financial gain for me unless I won the business. This conversation forced me to imagine a different way of working which is how I work to this day and I managed to remove all speculative meetings from my diary and replace them with productive work.

My planning session with Michael allowed my working hours to decrease whilst my income increased. This is not the magic of pyramid selling, this is the magic of being creative about your time — what you feel about it and how you invest it when you have a sense of purpose that is requiring you to make time available to it.

3. Go to Candy Morris's store on Saturday morning to buy some kit

I still go to Candy and Billy Morris's store, Woodland Enterprises, in Great Shefford when I need to buy some kit. She and Billy became friends of mine and we ended up living in the same village, East Garston. Candy introduced me to her brother, Gary Moore, the brilliant Brighton trainer who gave me a spin on the racetrack in a charity race on a horse called Theatre of Life (see Chapter 13) and for whom I rode out throughout 2007 whilst living in Brighton

4. Go to watch Martin Bosley's string work on the gallops

Former jockey and talented trainer, Martin Bosley, and his wife, the champion amateur jockey, Sarah Bosley not only became and remain great friends, but their patient nurturing along with their friendship and endless encouragement, played a massive role in helping me win my bet. Within three weeks of this meeting and my first lesson with Tina, Martin let me go up the gallops on Franklin Lakes, a beautiful and sensitive racehorse in full training, with Sarah behind shouting real time advice — and lots of it!

5. Go for an hour's riding lesson with Tina Fletcher

Tina Fletcher and Gee taught me to ride. I wouldn't say I was a great rider even today, but I still ride out and also ride each week with my daughter who has caught the bug. Always patient, always encouraging, always kind, Tina helped me build the good strong foundations for a pastime that I enjoy to this day but, critically, the foundations that would enable me to move at speed from novice to race riding.

Now you could say that all that was luck!

You could say that you couldn't pull that off — I certainly didn't think that I could. But the truth is that neither you nor I have to pull it off. And it isn't luck. The Ten Rules will pull it off for you if you use them to out-manoeuvre the Tiger. The Tiger that will tell you:

- "People like that don't want to speak to me."
- "My ideas won't interest other people."
- "I'll never be good enough to do it so I may as well not try."

And countless other Rule 2 'rules' designed to stop you from using the Ten Rules, taking the bold action, taking a small risk to go and win your prize.

Imagining the place where you want to be

Okay, enough sitting back in that chair. I know you've been thinking, dreaming and wondering. Having met a great many of you at events around the world, I also know that you may number among those people who are still looking for the catch, still desperate to believe that it cannot be done and that you should therefore be let off the hook from trying.

Now I'm going to ask you to plan. If now isn't a good time for you to do planning, please take your diary out and look for the next available time that is. Whatever time of the day, wherever in the world you might be at that time, find a place for it in your diary now. And bear in mind that if you take this appointment with yourself out of your diary because you are letting some Short Term-Low Risk time investment (that's the noise of life and work, basically — see Rule 8) take priority, you are committing a terrible sin. This planning session is the rock that you should be building everything else upon, not the other way around.

A question for you: When do we normally put 'goals' down on a piece of paper?

You've got it. For most of the Western world it is 1st January. So, after a really late night, a few weeks of over-indulgence during the festival period and, quite possibly, with the most severe hangover you will have in any twelve month stretch, you sit down and start planning the 'new you' with the help of endless supplements and magazines. It is no real wonder that the monk-like pledges of sobriety and abstinence that we make on 1st January last until around about 7th January. They're not driven by a sense of purpose, they're driven by a sense of guilt, and guilt is not a good foundation for imagining a bright new future and exciting new adventures.

So, instead of feeling guilty about all the over-indulgence that's left you many pounds overweight, a more exciting, and probably more effective, way of thinking is to think of things you'd like to do. Few of them will allow you to continue to eat badly or ignore your body's need to take exercise. By discovering a sense of purpose, it is likely that you will find yourself deciding to treat your body well.

Now when you are dreaming and imagining and creating the place that you want to arrive at, start off with as large a canvas as you like. Don't let anything get in the way of your initial thought processes. Don't judge, don't rely on your Rulebook to tell you what you can and cannot do.

Now don't worry, I'm not about to change hats and start telling you that "you can do anything — all you've got to do is dream, repeat my mantra and work at it every day." I don't believe that. I don't think the people who say things like that believe it either. But I do certainly think that this initial phase should be a big, broad canvas and that, for most of us, the problem is not starting with too wild an idea, it's starting with a too small an idea.

We're not going to spend a lot of time here thinking about 'aligning yourself with your core values' and 'discovering who you really are', there are books enough out there to guide you through those sorts of processes if you'd like that help. I'm going to gamble that you know in your heart of hearts what it is you want to be getting on with in the next chapter of your life. What we're interested in is getting you started on actually writing it.

So, when you have the beginnings of a place where you want to be, apply that test that we looked at back in Chapter 5, when we looked at Rule 2. Write down all the reasons why *you know* that you will not be able to achieve the things that you have just imagined. And then go through them one by one, ideally with a good friend, perhaps with a stranger in a coffee shop who looks interesting, but most of all with any-one other than somebody who is going to be motivated to find reasons to support your Rulebook. Give this person the job of helping you to decide which of the rules can be scien-tifically proven and which of them have perhaps been keeping you safe from taking little risks for many, many years and should be modified immediately.

It's an intriguing exercise. Good luck!

Putting the plan in place

When you begin to write your plan — how you are going to move every single day towards the place that you want to be — it is tempting just to put down 'work', the grind, the things that will have to be done to get there. But it's vital as you do this to look at things you can enjoy during this process. Getting up at 5am and going to sit on a horse isn't always inspiring at 10pm when you turn off the lights. And it would be easy on some mornings to feel glum getting out of bed. But if you focus instead on the feeling of elation as you finish a fast and well executed piece of work at the top of a hill in the Berkshire Downs at 7am on a crisp autumnal morning, and watch the steam rising from your horse's neck and from his breath and look out over the frosty landscape beneath you, as you strike up a conversation with a good friend sitting up beside you, things ain't so bad!

Here are some solid, practical steps that you can use to help you create a powerful plan that will take you, every single day, in the direction of where you want to arrive:

Step one: Look for what will bring you down

Look carefully, think carefully, imagine carefully. What is it that will really make this project grind to a halt? For me, as Michael pointed it out, it would be having to spend fifty hours a week bringing home the bacon. If I didn't deal with that, there would be no point starting on the project. This was a fascinating starting place for me. I was still stuck on the idea that a lack of any ability to ride a horse would be the stumbling block. Michael didn't have any worries about that. He was worried that I wouldn't have enough time to learn in the first place. And he was right.

So get real. Get real in this planning process and begin to look at what's going to bring you down. Is it the commute? Is it lack of support from your family? Is it how you fit it alongside your working life? Is it getting the boss onside? These are not reasons to give up. They are things that you'll need to deal with early on. Let's get them onto the plan now!

Step two: Use the Rules for Taming Tigers

You will find the answers to how to deal with the issues posed above within the covers of this book. They may not be explicit; but they are there. You'll find them within the covers of this book because either I came up against similar on the way to the racetrack or the great Tiger tamers whose stories are told in this book came up against them on the way to achieving their goals. Everything that you read about in these pages has been written by practitioners rather than by theorists. You can lean on what is being said here, you can trust it and you can adapt it to your world.

Step three: Write down disciplines

You will need to put in place certain things that you will do every day — these will be your new disciplines — to reach an exciting new place. So important did I realise that this was to the racing year that it became Rule 9 (there were only eight when I took the bet). You can read about discipline in Chapter 12.

Step four: Write down the 'why'

Why are you doing this? What are you going to get out of it? When you are there, in the moment, thinking of cheating on one of your disciplines or giving up the project altogether, what's the big reason that you can look at in your mind to encourage you to stay on track?

In any kind of change, knowing the 'why' is absolutely vital. For my money, this is where most corporate change programmes fall down. Too much 'what', 'how' and 'when' broadcast out to a willing but battered audience. The 'why' is constantly forgotten as command and control overrides inspiration and motivation and engagement. Don't fall into that trap. That is why the New Year resolutions fail. How are you going to motivate, inspire and engage yourself when the going gets tough?

Step five: Diarise it

It's meaningless on a piece of paper, it needs to be in your diary, and these elements of your plan need to be the least movable feasts that you place there. Here you are writing the story of your life, writing the next chapter. Here you've grasped the pen back from the Tiger. Don't let a meeting with a grumpy customer knock this bit out of your diary. Knock something else out first if you really have to let the customer in.

Step six: Plan a bold action

The final step, if you have not already completed this after the challenge laid down in Chapter 4, is to plan your bold action for today and to get the thing started. You have to get it started! And the bold action should involve somebody else, because that's where the Tigers are tamed. The bold action is not to go to the bookshop and buy a manual on your credit card. The bold action is to ring up somebody who could help you or to sit down with your partner and tell them what it is you would like to achieve and what it is you plan to do to get there and ask for their support.

You will know what the bold action is because it's the thing that you least want to do and yet the thing that is most likely to take you there. Do it today if possible, and if not, before 10am tomorrow morning.

Step seven: Now do something

Enough said.

Rule 3 is the last of the Integrity Rules. If you have followed Rules 1–3, then you have now met the Tiger and reflected on its impact on the integrity of your story to date. You have examined some of the rules that you use to keep yourself safe and imagined what the world would be like if these were edited to be more in tune with reality. You have imagined a place that you would like to arrive at, you have thought about your sense of purpose and you may have a plan to act in accordance with your desire to get there.

Now actions can be in integrity with desires and not safety.

Over to you.

Case study: Christine Lea

Around six or seven years ago, my life turned upside down. My husband left and my mother, whom I had been looking after for some years, died. I had been a primary school teacher for a number of years but my job had started to feel stale. I was not happy at all and felt that something had to change. I came across Jim's Ten Rules for Taming Tigers when I picked up one of his cards and everything started from there.

I started to follow the Rules and facing up to my Tigers. I found that what had been holding me back, my Tigers, was fear of an unknown place, both in terms of my career and my personal life — a fear of starting again. I was afraid of putting myself among new people and presenting myself to them. I found that Rule 3, 'Head in the direction of where you want to arrive — every single day', was particularly useful to me. I had to take things one step at a time.

"I was afraid of putting myself among new people and presenting myself to them. I found that Rule 3 was particularly useful to me — I had to take things one step at a time."

I left primary school teaching and got a job lecturing on Early Years Education at a university. It was quite a challenge embarking on a new career in my sixties and I had to adapt from teaching small children to teaching people aged mainly somewhere between their late twenties and early fifties, many of whom were embarking on a new career themselves. It wasn't always easy finding the right mood for lectures to adults when I was so used to teaching children. The point I felt that I had really committed, when I knew that I had done the right thing, was during a lecture I was teaching. Up to then, I had been sticking rigidly to my lecture plans, largely because it was working. On this day, I took a risk and tried something different, without sticking to my plan, and I discovered that it worked even better.

Wimbledon College, a big London state school. Some good things. Some bad things. No horses.

I trained and began my practice at SJ Berwin & Co in London. Still no horses.

12 stones of me enjoying the local hospitality with Maddie in Blackrock, Ireland before the bet.

Gee.

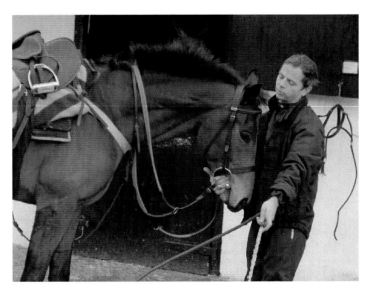

With Airgusta at Charlie Morlock's yard in Kingston Lisle.

Martin and Sarah Bosley at the office.

A left-handed handshake at Brighton. The right is not working anymore!

First Race. Airgusta and I are number 10, white colours against the rails.

We did it!

Playing with the crowd in
Barcelona.

Speaking in London at 8st 10lbs,
the lightest I got to.

Finally starting to get the hang of it. Riding work upsides Richard Dunwoody for Roger Ingram at his Open Day. Epsom, May 2008.

Peter Winters   Chris Pierce

Katrina Dunkley

Paul Croft

Isobel Ryder

Lotta Vilde Wahl

I found that as I made changes in my career, other areas of my life changed too. I have become more determined in my attitude, my social life has changed and I have a new group of friends. I am eating more healthily and taking regular exercise. If anyone had suggested to me ten years ago that I would have made so many changes, I would have smiled behind my hand!

Sometimes I have wanted to give up, or thought that all the changes are more than I can cope with but I decided instead to tackle the Tigers and try and see why I felt like that.

Through my course, I have recommended Jim's approach to others and have set others off working on their Tigers. I still try to do something scary every day, sometimes it's something administrative, sometimes a people matter, sometimes a student with a problem. I have found that it really works for me.

Part Three

The Leadership Rules

Chapter 7

Rule 4: It's all in the mind

The first Leadership rule

Now, as we discussed, Rules 1–3 are called the Integrity Rules because, for many people, it is the first time they have been able to act or begin contemplating acting in integrity with what they believe they should and could be doing. In the Integrity Rules, the Tiger is revealed (Rule 1), the 'blame' is removed from others and placed on our own shoulders as we recognize that we're the one creating the rules and we are the ones writing the story (Rule 2), and a new possibility is imagined and a plan created to achieve it (Rule 3). Now we are beginning to act in integrity with ourselves.

Rules 4, 5 and 6 are about leadership. As a first step, this is about leading ourselves rather than permitting the Tiger to lead us, but then it is about beginning to lead others; seeing how our thoughts, words and actions can inspire others and, if necessary, can also bring others to support the cause that we are now promoting and fighting for.

We shall discuss the Change Rules, Rules 7, 8 and 9 later in the book, but leadership, by definition, comes before change. Someone needs to provide the direction — preferably somebody who's acting in complete integrity — and somebody needs to be challenging the status quo, looking at the Rulebook — be that within the community, the company, the family or within the individual themselves — and spotting the possibilities for a change for the better.

This leader needs to be leading their own head, rather than being led by fear and their instinctive desire to avoid the things that cause the fear (Rule 4). This leader will need to be able to truly value, on a deep level, the input of others and to respect others deeply, recognizing that their story will be by far the poorer if they're not working in concert with other people to achieve the desired changes (Rule 5). And this leader will need to have the courage to stand alone, to move away from the pack, to state out loud who they are and what they stand for (Rule 6). There's no greater time for a Tiger to attack than when you are considering a move away from the pack, which is why Rule 1 is there, and why Rule 10 is there, because it's never going to get any easier, and a decision to give up will stay with you for many, many years to come.

And, according to the Rules for taming Tigers, all of these Integrity Rules and Leadership Rules will need to be attended to, reflected upon and acted upon before the big change can take place, before the new order can be consolidated, made consistent and even used as a springboard to the next challenge to the Tiger.

The voices

Do you hear voices in your head?

I certainly do. And if you think that you don't, the voice that I'm referring to is the voice that you're now having a conversation with saying:

"Hmm, I wonder if I do hear voices?"

"Don't be ridiculous!"

"No, really, do we hear voices?"

"What's this 'we' business?"

Okay, let's try this from a different direction. Have you ever stood up in front of a group to speak, whether at work, at home, or at college? As you stood in front of that group, did you have a voice in your head saying to you, "Man, you are hot. They love you, look! They are hanging on your every word!"? Or did you have a voice in your head saying, "Man, you are really crap. You'd better get this done as quickly as possible and sit down fast. They're looking at you like you are a total muppet!"?

Personally, I've always had a problem with the second voice. I very rarely get to meet the first one.

Now, let's just say for a moment that this voice that sits on your shoulder and puts you off doing things, or criticises you whilst you are in the middle of doing things, is the Tiger's voice. Let's just consider together how many times a day that Tiger's voice, that horrible, roaring, meanest manifestation of the Tiger, dictates an action to you, makes the choice for you. Let's just suppose for a moment that the voice in your head talks you out of doing something that you'd quite like to do five times a day. You might think that that's a lot, perhaps many more times than would apply to you. And if that is the case, many congratulations.

But you should be sure before you pat yourself on the back. Notice that voice the next time you think of asking a vital question in a large group, speaking to an interesting person that you would like to speak to, or when you find yourself pulling back from making a bold statement, diluting it as it comes out of your mouth. Notice it the next time you move from striking out with full commitment to achieve a result in the moment to hobbling along in luscious mediocrity as a result of this voice. Notice it before you decide that this chapter doesn't apply to you.

And let's think on. If this voice dictates our actions, influences and even dominates our choices five times in one day, how many times is that a week? Well, let's rest on 35. How many times is that in a year? 1,820.

We began this book by asking who was writing the story of our lives, by asking whether we are writing the story that we wish to write and are fully able to write or whether we are permitting the Tiger to dictate the story to us. Let's just say for argument's sake that we will have seventy years during which we can impact on the world around us. Seventy years, let's say from the age of ten to eighty (probably too young, but for argument's sake) when we can make the choices that will create the story that will be ours. Now if we multiply 1,820 by 70 we get to an incredible 124,400.

That's 124,400 times in our lives when the Tiger has dictated the choice to us rather than us making the choice, doing the thing that we actually want to do, that we believe we should do, that we know we probably can do.

You and I have already explored the idea that where we are today, in most aspects of our lives, is the sum of the choices we have made to date. From what career we chose to what we've chosen to eat to whether or not to take exercise or smoke cigarettes to which attractive people we chose to speak with and which to ignore. We made our choices. We got our outcomes. We are where we are.

So let me ask you again before we go into this chapter any further:

Who is writing the story of your life? You? Or the Tiger?

It's your voice

Now, when you were presenting to that group earlier, and the voice came along to give you a little live critique of your performance, you were not visited by the god of real time presentation skills feedback. If there is any little piece of you that thinks that you were, the assistance you need is not to be found in the pages of this book. So if you are not actually hearing voices from outside, from some supernatural force, then where is this critique coming from?

Of course it's you, your voice. It was always your voice. And because it's your voice, that means you can change it to say things that will help you. Perhaps by listening to CDs promising to 'reprogram your mind'. Or perhaps not. Perhaps by working carefully, like an elite sportsperson or businessperson would do, to train yourself to perform better under pressure. Because the voice only ever attacks when we are under pressure, doesn't it? Whether that pressure is real and immediate and felt right there in the moment, in front of the audience or whether it is imagined, felt when we are sitting quietly, in a place of safety, merely thinking about a scenario that would place us under pressure and challenge the Tiger.

Later in this chapter I will work with you to develop strategies to deal with this voice. It's important, it's not to be taken lightly, but it is perfectly possible to change the way it works for you. First, though, I would like to look at this voice in a little bit more detail with you. Let's try to understand what's happening here. Let's try to increase your awareness of this voice and of how frequently and how importantly it does, or does not, dictate to you the action that you should take, and make your choice for you.

The voice in our head that nudges us towards the path of least resistance, the path that keeps us within the safety zone is simply the result of fear. Generally, it is merely fear of the unknown. It is uncertainty. When we don't know what will happen in a certain situation, it causes us alarm, and when we experience this alarm it causes us fear, and when we experience fear the voice will criticise us (we will examine this process more closely when we consider Rule 7).

We know that we can avoid this discomfort if we listen to the little voice.

So, whilst we are presenting to the group, faced with an incredible opportunity to make an impact, to raise our profile, to secure something exciting today, we find ourselves reducing our commitment and our energy and our enthusiasm as the voice tells us to retreat back into our little shell, just in case it goes wrong.

So, as we sit in private late at night with a piece of paper in front of us on the dining room table, and consider putting forward that exciting new idea, the little voice persuades us that we will be ridiculed if we were to propose it and so it remains sitting on a scrap of paper until it eventually finds its way into the recycling bin.

And if you can relate to any of those feelings, then I am sure you will see that, as long as this voice is unchecked in its influence upon you, you will always opt for the path of least resistance. You are like a river being forced this way and then that by rocks but, unlike those which guide the path of the river, your rocks are illusions, are imaginary and should not be permitted to dictate your path.

The voice is, indeed, related to the Rulebook. But it is different. The Rulebook is how we view the world and view our place in the world and our ability (or lack of ability) to influence that world. The Rulebook often seems perfectly rational and intellectually certain until we take the time to challenge it rationally. Our battle with the voice is live! It is our 'in the moment' struggle with the Tiger whenever we face a moment of fear, be that because of a challenge to a rule in our Rulebook or some other challenge.

Now, if you think for one moment that you are so special that the Tiger only attacks *you* in this way, think again. If you're sitting anywhere near a computer, search for the phrase "sports psychology". Have a little look at how many pages are dedicated, in part, to dealing with the voice when the pressure is on. It's one thing to sink a four metre putt on a nice flat green when you are all alone. It's quite another thing with a competitor standing opposite you. It's another thing again if there's a bet of a thousand pounds riding between the two of you. And it's something else yet again when it's a putt to win the US Open being broadcast live around the world. And as the pressure mounts, so does the little voice.

And if all those sportsmen and women and, indeed, everybody else who puts themselves under pressure out there on a daily basis can deal with the voice, so can you.

Cantering to post

The voices were so intense in my head at the thought of my first race, that it did cross my mind at 3.30am one morning in the week before my first race that if I stood up in the saddle whilst I was in the starting stalls and reached up high, I would be able to put my fingers through the wire mesh at the top of the stalls. And if I held on tight, then when the starter opened the gates and the horse jumped off into a gallop, I could be left behind to climb down to the ground beneath me and stroll home in one piece.

Now, if I were reading that, I guess I would be saying to myself , "Oh, come on, Jim, it's only riding a horse for heaven's sake." And of course, I'd be right. This wasn't brain surgery — it wasn't as clever and it certainly wasn't as scary as that would be — but it was enough to get my voice chattering pretty loudly, I have to confess. So perhaps I should explain why.

You see, a jockey's first job is to get his horse to the starting stalls, and then to stop when he gets there. This, of course, must sound like pretty basic stuff to the non-rider of racehorses — just apply the brakes when you get near to the start. But there is one big design fault in the thoroughbred racehorse: No brakes! It's all just a negotiation; you ask nicely and you hope it'll stop. Better jockeys than me (and you won't have to look far to find one of those) may well argue that they have perfected the art of pulling up the race-horse. But just ask them when the last time was that they got run away with on the gallops or on the racetrack and they'll probably start to look a little sheepish. And if they can get run away with, you bet your life this new boy can. And where better to do it than cantering to post on the first time you've taken a horse onto a racecourse?

As I was being led down the chute by Caroline Grimes at Southwell Racecourse on the 22nd November 2004. My mount, Airgusta was certainly on his toes and looking for-ward to getting his hooves onto the sand. As we got to the track, we had to turn left and canter past the grandstand before pulling up as we passed the crowd, doing a U-turn and cantering back to post. Excellent. Two opportunities to fail to pull the thing up!

As I cantered past the grandstand, which I had planned for and thought about in my mind's eye, the commentator began to talk. Now this I had not planned for or prepared for in my mind's ear.

"And cantering down now past us we have No. Ten, Airgusta, ridden today by Jim Lawless. Jim is having his first ride here at Southwell Racecourse this afternoon, and, for those of you who have not read today's Racing Post, you may like to know that Jim has only been riding horses for just twelve months. So now is not the time to visit the bar, ladies and gentlemen. Things could be about to get extremely interesting out here on the track!"

The voice was getting louder, "I hope I can reach the top of the starting stalls."

Airgusta was very kind to me. We took a steady canter to
the starting stalls and pulled up nicely, but the voice hadn't
gone away just yet, "All I've done so far is ride a horse to the
starting stalls, although it does feel like a big relief to be
here." We walk around 'taking a turn' with all of the other
horses waiting for the stalls handlers to load us.

Now you should realise at this stage that once loading
begins it happens quickly and efficiently. When you're in the
starting stalls it's an intimidating place for the novice.
You're locked up in a coffin-shaped steel cage with half a ton
of really wound-up pure equine muscle. The stalls are very
narrow and your feet and legs are touching each side. If the
horses buck or kick or try to escape beneath the gates at the
front of the stalls, things can escalate very quickly into a difficult situation, so the stalls handlers and the starter are keen
to load and release the field as quickly and safely as they can.

What they do not do as they load down at the start of a
horserace is have the starter call out, "Are you ready, boys?
Are you steady? Wait for it, wait for it. Go!"

No, it's slightly more brutal and urgent than that down
there. As the stalls handlers load each horse in they call out,
"Ten to load, nine to load, eight to load." As the last horse is
loaded in the final stalls, the stalls handler clears the front of
the gates and signals to the starter that all the horses are
loaded.

The starter calls out, "Jockeys," drops his flag and the
gates are opened. And you move from nought to thirty miles
an hour in around twenty-five yards. My main focus at this
stage was to still be on Airgusta's back in twenty-five yards'
time, and not lying on the floor of the stall Number One
wondering what on Earth had just happened to me. So it was

imperative that I was sitting balanced on the horse and ready for the acceleration — which I had been warned would be so much faster than anything I'd experienced in the practice stalls at the yard — as soon as the starter pressed his button. My eyes were glued to the hand holding the flag as I listened to the stalls handlers count down the horses left to load.

The voice in my head at this stage was not doing me any favours. All I could think about was falling off the thing or jabbing Airgusta in the mouth with the reins by having too tight a hold as he leapt forward. But the voices got a lot louder when, just as they announced that there were only two horses left to load, I saw not one but two ambulances, pulling up behind the starter!

I knew that one ambulance was required to be there for Health & Safety regulations at the track, but my voice immediately told me, "the second ambulance is here because they've read that some idiot who has only been riding for a year is about to take part in the race." This was my last thought as the gates opened and Airgusta cruised, beautifully, to the position at the front of the field, up against the inside rail, which I'd agreed with his trainer, Charlie Morlock.

The types of voices in our heads

There are two types of voices that the Tiger will use to roar at us in an attempt to dictate our stories to us.

The first is the voice that attacks us 'in the moment'. It attacks us whilst we are doing something, causing us to either lose focus momentarily or, worse, to pull back from giving something our best shot and give it a second rate shot instead. Let's stick with the idea of a presentation here — in front of any group, at home or at work — because it will probably ring a loud bell with most people. That voice is there, draining your confidence, live in front of the audience, demanding that you scale down your passion and commitment and, instead, substitute a mediocre performance of the kind that everybody else always gives.

The second voice, although perhaps less immediately identifiable to you, is what we shall call the 'anticipatory voice'. This is the voice which can masquerade as the voice of reason or commonsense when we are lying in the dead of night worrying about a particular situation or whether we should take a particular course. It is the voice that says to you, "They're right, they're all right. Who the hell do you think you are to try to ride in a horserace / marry this person / get a promotion / change the way your company operates / pass the exam / start your own successful small business?"

Doing battle with the voices

There are four main ways to do battle with the voices and to ensure that you are entirely in control of your own mind, rather than the Tiger, when taking your decisions, in the moment or in anticipation.

Tool one: Evidence

You will know by now that we are not into 'shortcuts' around here. This is because shortcuts don't often work unless you are physically travelling from A to B. If you have evidence in your head to suggest that what you are about to do is going to go horribly wrong, you will have fear in your mind — the voices will go crazy. It is very important to realise that this is not a fictional Tiger giving you a hard time, it is commonsense saying to you that you are not ready to take on the challenge you are about to face.

If somebody handed me the keys to a shiny new Boeing 747 and said that they would pay me ten million pounds to fly it from London Heathrow to JFK and I agreed, the voices would be kicking off with all the power of a football crowd as I took my seat in the cockpit.

If you don't know what you are doing, get training. How many people live their lives in terror of presenting to an audience and yet never go and get a couple of days training in this perfectly learnable skill? How many people spend their lives not daring to start their own business because they don't understand accounts?

So seek out evidence that you can perform the thing well — earn that evidence if necessary. Get the training. Ask for the advice. Get the mentoring. Do the rehearsal. Have dry runs. Do whatever it takes to ensure that when you stand up there you can do the thing well. List all of these things that you have done on a piece of paper and look at them and marvel at yourself.

And do not expect any of this to stop the voices from coming when you enter the fray. But what it will do for you is two things. Firstly, it will reduce the noise that the voices make as you stand before your nemesis. Secondly, as you stand there and they begin to take hold, you can fight back. You can recognise that this is a Tiger. You can recognise that it is your natural instinct kicking in to force you towards mediocrity and away from a wonderful result — a result that you were always capable of achieving, but that you have now put in the work to deserve to achieve. With a little experience, you will be able to stop the Tiger in its tracks.

Tool two: Build confidence

Now you could buy those same CDs that will give you instant confidence as you listen to them in your sleep. But this confuses me. Give you instant confidence in what? Your ability to hold a conversation with a beautiful stranger? Your ability to ride a horse at speed or fly a 747?

Think for a moment of the areas in which you would be willing to say that you are 'confident'. Has that confidence arisen as a result of reprogramming your mind subliminally? Or has it come about as a result of your willingness to put in the work? Has it arisen through your willingness to challenge the Rulebook (the route to all personal development) until you have the right (as bestowed by you, yourself) to create a new Rulebook that you can believe in (and let's call the possession of that new Rulebook "confidence")? Has your confidence arisen because you didn't give up when the going got tough? Has your confidence arisen because you went out day after day and practised the thing? If you're a parent, were you more confident on Week Fifty-two after the birth than you were on Week One? How did that arise? Was it reprogramming? Or was it practice, dedication, and persistence?

The more confident you are as you approach a challenge, the less the Tiger dares kick off the voice in your head.

But perhaps there is a flaw here. How can you be confident the *first* time you do this thing? The answer is that you won't be. Or, at least, you won't be as confident as you will become. This is the time to rely upon Tool One, building up evidence to do battle with the voices before you go into the room — all that training, all those dry runs. Building enough evidence to begin to feel as though you have some right to be 'confident' of getting through. And this also is the time for looking to Tool Three.

Tool three: The task in hand

Now here's a thing. When we focus on the task at hand rather than on how well we may or may not be doing at performing that task, the voices disappear and we start to perform far better.

Let's go through that again, and let's use the presentation room again as it is a common place for fear to be felt and voices to make themselves heard.

When you stand in front of your friends and tell them a funny story, the voices don't appear in your head. You are lost in the task at hand. You have no little critique in your head undermining your confidence in real time as you stand in front of them. What did you do with your hands? How did you use your voice? You will never know and you will never care. You were absorbed in the task and not on such irrelevances. All that matters is that your friends enjoyed the story and laughed, and the evening went on merrily.

When we present to the board, when we talk to a group of strangers, we begin to ask ourselves irrelevant questions. We begin to ask ourselves, "How am I doing? Do they like how I look? Can they see that I'm nervous? Am I speaking in a boring voice? Will I forget my . . . Doh!"

And then we are sunk.

Now, let's imagine that you have been told by an evil gangster that something very unpleasant is going to happen to you if you don't manage to persuade the room to move in a certain direction by the time you've finished presenting. Are you worried about whether they like you now? Are you giving much thought to what your hands are doing, or whether you have too many bullet points on a PowerPoint slide? Oh, no. Now you're engaged in the task at hand, and so am I! Just watch us draw them in with our eye contact and our confident stance as we immerse ourselves in the job of persuading them to come with us rather than immersing ourselves in the lovely self-indulgence of critiquing ourselves.

Jump jockeys are very interesting on this subject. If the voice gets hold of them midway through a race, the horse will sense the fear and doubt and begin to share it. And a horse sensing and then feeling fear and doubt is not a horse you want to sit on as it approaches a large jump at speed. They talk about being so immersed in the task at hand that they "throw their heart over the fence and the horse will follow." Their whole mind is occupied with nursing the horse over the jump in the right stride, at the right pace, with the right distribution of weight so that they can take off quickly as they land on the other side. There's little time for self-criticism and there is no place for it — until the race is over.

So, the next time the voice is giving you a hard time and you have worked on creating the evidence as to why you have the right to carry out this task successfully, and you have worked on your confidence, stop being so self-indulgent! Get on with the job and the thing will take care of itself.

Tool Four: Mental rehearsal

I had never been a fan of mental rehearsal until it came to preparing for my first race. I used it to help me get through those starting stalls, and I do believe it is the reason that I didn't cling on to the top of the stalls and let the horse kick on without me.

Here's the idea. You run through the event, as you want it to occur, in your mind's eye and with as much detail attached as possible. You work on it going well, you work on the detail of what you are doing that makes it go well, you work on being lost in the task itself and you work on enjoying the sensation, watching the result unfold and enjoying the success.

They're beginning to write books on the subject, enjoy them by all means, but in essence it is simple. Find a quiet place, close your eyes, run the thing through your head in as much detail as you can and work on the points above.

Let me tell you why this was so important to me in the run up to my first race. I was scared, very scared of two things as the race approached. So scared, in fact, that I would wake up at 4am and lie in bed rehearsing them going wrong in my mind and becoming more anxious as I saw all the many and varied possibilities for me failing.

The two things that I was really nervous about were sitting in / jumping out from the stalls, and not getting bolted with as a result of the horse sensing my nerves as we began to canter down towards the start. I was working on finding the evidence, I was working on building confidence, I was concerned that I wouldn't be able to concentrate on the task at hand, despite this, and that the voices would still get the better of me.

So I went to speak to Michael Caulfield, whom we met in Chapter 1 and who, by now, had moved fulltime into his new profession of sports psychologist and was already achieving some great results. It was Michael who persuaded me to use mental rehearsal. Not as a shortcut, I must stress — mentally rehearsing that flight in the 747 is not going to help me or my passengers — but as an additional tool. Now I had been through the starting stalls at home, of course, many times in preparation. I had been through the starting stalls at the British Racing School in Newmarket under expert guidance, and been videoed in the process. But, as Michael pointed out, I had not been through the starting stalls on a racetrack.

He advised me to go racing as many times as I could over the next week, and to go to the start of every single race. He advised me to listen to what the stalls handlers shouted, to look at how they moved, to look at the order in which they loaded the horses according to the draw, to listen to what the starter said, to watch how tight the jockey and horses were in the stalls and how little room there was for manoeuvre, and to watch the field jockeying for its positions as they belted off having left the stalls.

So I did this and, armed with all the new colours that this gave me, my imagination was able to partially rehearse going through the stalls on a racetrack.

Of course, I went there without real confidence — you can't have very much confidence in your ability to do something that you've never done before — but I did go there with lots of evidence to say that I should be able to go through. And I did go there having been successfully through the stalls many tens of times in my mind's eye. We jumped out nicely and I managed to get the position that Charlie had instructed me to get. Confidence rising. Voices calming.

124,400.

We are writing the story of our lives, that's for sure. Are we choosing the words though, or is our Tiger dictating them? If that voice tempers our actions five times a day then we calculated around 124,400 actions that are dictated by the Tiger.

Who do you want to write your story?

Over to you.

Case study: Isobel Ryder

My story really starts when I was two and taken into care. A couple of children's homes followed before I was fostered by a very nice family at the age of eleven until I was fifteen when I returned to live with my mum — this had a catastrophic affect on my education. I joined the army at eighteen with the grand total of three GCSEs. Various jobs followed including a spell with a private defence company and a well known confectionery company. On a personal front, I got married and had my daughter who has given me the opportunity to understand and give to her the mother-daughter relationship perhaps I should have had.

> *"So I got those Tigers off my back. I got focused. I decided I had nothing to lose by trying but everything to lose by quitting. I ultimately had three people to do it for, my mum, my daughter and myself."*

From September 2002 to February 2004 I completed an HNC in Business getting distinctions in most of my assignments, I was working fulltime; I loved my job and my life. It was always my intention to go on and get a degree to enhance my employment prospects and prove something to myself.

I then had to put my education on hold whilst the ensuing dramas unfolded around me. In March 2004, my mum was diagnosed with a terminal illness and my husband ended our marriage all in the space of forty-eight hours. I continued to work fulltime, had sole care of my daughter and tried to ensure my mum and I covered every unsaid misunderstanding in the time she had left. It was a particularly difficult year as I would have turned to my mum for support over my marriage and my husband for support regarding my mum — however I found, of course, I could not turn to either. I still sorely miss my mum and on the night she died, at her instruction, my sister-in-law gave me a picture of my mum getting her degree at fifty-six years of age.

As I moved into my own home with my daughter and in March 2006 I was made redundant — every life changing event that could happen seemed to have happened to me in the space of two years.

However, in the preceding August, my employer had run a 'Careers Workshop' day which had got me re-thinking about my education with a view to picking up where I had left off. Initially I thought I had lost the opportunity to further my education but on reflection the choice was mine. I went on holiday to Australia to visit my foster parents and decided to enrol on the Masters in Personnel and Development on my return using the redundancy money. I undertook a part-time, fixed term contract post to help with living costs.

The next two years were a roller-coaster of temporary employment, emotional and intellectual challenges but it was towards the end of the course that 'Taming Tigers' entered my life. I had always suffered from self-doubt and insecurity — I'm sure psychologists would put this down to the lack of parental support and encouragement during my early development years. I was trying to complete my dissertation. I had never done anything like this before, let alone at this level and on this scale. I was scared, feeling out of my depth and convincing myself that I had taken on too much — no one would blame me for opting out, surely. I was looking for excuses to drop out or delay completion for a year despite the support and encouragement from my programme manager and close friends — what did they know? I obviously wasn't going to pass, I had no A-Levels or first degree, who was I kidding?

At a local careers conference, I listened to Jim Lawless give his talk on 'Taming Tigers'; these voices telling me I was not going to make it, I was doomed to fail, bitten off more than I could chew etc. I was particularly impressed by the comment that the Grand

National doesn't change its date just because a particular jockey may not feel up to it that day — tough! Prepare and be ready or miss the opportunity, you may not win the race but taking part means you tried and can be proud the hard work was not wasted.

My mum's photograph has been on the wall behind me as I studied during the programme. I truly believe she knew what she was doing when she requested I had this picture — she was telling me to go for it. So I got those Tigers off my back. Because my dissertation was driven by two deadlines, the school year and the date for submission, I got focused (I decided I had nothing to lose by trying but everything to lose by quitting (financial, self-esteem and pride)). I ultimately had three people to do it for, my mum, my daughter and myself.

More recently I have acquired a new, fulltime, higher level (and pay) post and my life is progressing in leaps and bounds — I am heading in the direction I wanted to go.

As I look back over my life, I realise I am a fighter and a survivor and have been dealing with Tigers all my life — I just didn't know that's what they were called. I also believe in fate, Jim's talk on Taming Tigers came into my life at that point for a reason. It turned me around, stopped me feeling sorry for myself and although I am still awaiting the results, I believe I did enough to pass and hope to graduate in December when I know my mum will be watching.

[Editor's note: As we went to press we heard that Isobel has passed her Masters Degree].

Chapter 8

Rule 5: The Tools for Taming Tigers are all around you

This is a very exciting Chapter. The second of the Leadership Rules is this:

The tools for Taming Tigers are all around you.

As we go into this rule, you will stop believing me. We will have a little blip in our relationship of trust. I will try to win you back with a racing tale or two, and then, finally, I will ask you a killer question. And I'm hoping that by the time I do that, you will have come back to me, repaired the doubt and we'll be flying again.

And if I succeed, and you do decide to use this Rule to help you tame your Tiger and write your next chapter, extraordinary results will follow. So, here goes.

Dependence

We start life as dependent creatures. We cannot survive without another caring enough to feed us, clothe us and even deal with our wastes. I don't know about you, but as I grew to the stage where I could deal with the latter aspects but was still reliant on my parents to feed and clothe me, I began to get pretty impatient for the next phase: 'Independence'.

When would I be out there on my own?

Independence

The thrill of the word! And not just the word but the excitement of experiencing it, the freedom, the ability to come home at a time of your choosing, to a place that you own the front door key to, with another person beside you who is attracted to you.

And as a young lawyer, this word was particularly important to me at work and, so far as I could see, to my colleagues also. We were in a rush to prove that we needed nobody else around. We were certainly in a rush to prove that we did not need other lawyers watching over us. And I guess that by my mid-twenties I had finally achieved some level of independence at work and outside of work — enough to make me feel free.

But of course, I was not free. I had found a new prison. A prison surrounded by Tigers. A prison called me. A freedom of ambition defined merely by my independent imagination. A freedom to act defined merely by my independent level of courage. A pace of execution defined merely by my independent ability to get on with getting things done. In retrospect, independence has its limitations.

Of course, I had no idea that life had another level on this particular growth adventure. Having given little thought to leadership, either in a work or an out-of-work capacity,

I had not given any thought to the tremendous thrill, responsibility, joy and terror of genuinely throwing my lot in with that of another, or others.

I was a late developer in this area, for sure, but I got there. And when I got there I realised that I had misunderstood my own Rule. Rule 5 had always been an homage to teamwork, the power of people pulling together. I had drawn the line at ever uttering the phrase, "there is no I in team", but it was a close call for a while.

The reality dawned on me during one of my regular trips to Gee's office at AP's house to tell her how things were going at the yard, whether I had managed to follow my instructions precisely when riding, how I was doing with my weight, and then to tell the occasional white lie about how much running I had done in the course of that week (I would be rumbled, of course, when we next ran together and she belted off into the distance with a wry grin).

We chatted and she had a Diet Coke and some Minstrels, my very favourite chocolates. I had water and pinched three of the Champ's Jaffa Cakes when Gee wasn't looking. We went over how I was doing on the gallops. It was a marginal improvement on the week before but I confessed that I thought that was due more to the good mood of the horses than any 'magic' that had finally reached my hands. Finally, we agreed a time to visit Tina's together to have a session on the lunge rein so that we could work on my balance with stirrups short and without reins in walk, trot, and canter.

As I was about to head off to London for a meeting, Gee commented on how surprised she was that I was never scared by what she was asking me to do or the situations that our pace of progress was forcing me into. I remember pausing and thinking in detail about whether I should follow my gut instinct and give a bland answer or whether I should tell the whole truth. I told the truth.

"I'm terrified most of the time! Can't you tell?"

"What? You have to tell me if you are scared. I have to know!" She was almost angry. I had never seen her like this. I was astonished.

"Why?" I asked, instantly regretting my honesty.

"How can I possibly help you if I don't know what I need to help you with?"

Now forgive my slowness, but this was the first time that I began to appreciate that Gee was operating on a different level to me. Until then I had thought that she was skilled in her area and was passing that skill on to me. Now I realised that there was much more going on, that she knew things that I hadn't discovered, and that these things were not (directly at least) to do with horsemanship.

She was telling me that if I was not willing to be vulnerable enough to be honest with her about my weaknesses, she could not work with me as fast as she could otherwise. I was frustrating the project with my pride. But I had never told anybody about these things — my worries and fears, complete with cold sweats and everything. Surely she'd bail on me if she knew how pathetic I really was?

I was being what I had been so proud to become: 'Independent'. I had kept my cards to my chest. I needed to understand that next step: 'Interdependence'. I needed to show Gee my hand — twos and threes, as well as aces. I had to face a lot of Tigers about that, a lot of Tigers. But I tried to do it. And she helped me get to grip with things that worried me. And she didn't bail on me. Ever.

Interdependence

And that became the new understanding of Rule 5. It can be about Teams and Teamwork if you want it to be, but there is a glittering prize that is so much more appealing than a 'mere' team: moving that team, and ourselves, to Interdependence. Becoming vulnerable. Becoming part of, and even building, a truly great team with members' strengths recognised and cherished and weaknesses accepted.

A beginner's guide to Rule 5

Let's return to Interdependence in a moment. Let's get started with the basics of Rule 5 straight away.

Remember, Rule 5: 'The tools for Taming Tigers are all around you'. Whatever it is that you would like to start writing into your next chapter, the tools to assist you in doing that are all around you. Why don't you list them? I have no idea what they are for you. Maybe it is the brand that you have on your business card — have you ever thought of the power that that holds? Maybe it is the people you know at work, the experience that is sitting all around you but that the Tiger prevents you from displaying 'vulnerability' to. Maybe it is a friend of a friend that you have never met and you'll have to get on the phone to discover their very existence.

Maybe the tool for you is your creativity, your ingenuity, your communication skills, your education, your mum, the meeting you have with somebody this afternoon that you could add a new element to and gain some new insights from.

Whatever it is you want to write in the next chapter, the
tools for taming that Tiger and getting it done are all
around you. Maybe you are holding one tool in your hand
right now and reading it. I don't know. But I promise you
that *you* do.

Think!

During the course of this book you have been thinking about
the things that you haven't done and that you have now
missed out on — opportunities that are no longer there and
that the Tiger stole from you. But the tools were always
there to help you.

During the course of this book, you have also been thinking about the things that you should be getting on with now.
What you will write into the next chapter of your story.
During the course of this book, you have decided to do
things and the Tiger has already stopped you from doing
them. (Oh, I'm sorry. Maybe it wasn't the Tiger. Maybe you
really have been, genuinely, too busy, twenty-four/seven, to
do that bold action you came up with in Chapter 4. My mistake!) Please don't let the Tiger waste another sentence of
your story!

Use Rule 5 to get things going.

Let's just work with people as the 'tool' for a moment. Think
of the person that you need to help you — the most outra-
geous, powerful, perhaps even apparently unattainable person who could help you to get done what you want to get
done, or at least get started.

Now call them up. They are waiting for your call!

Now I promised that we would fall out during this chapter, that I would stretch your confidence and lose you. This is that part. If your confidence is not being stretched, then I guess you are already on the phone. If you are unsure, then think about it for a moment before you skip this chapter in a huff.

People are the most thrilling tool to getting things done. They are brilliant things. We underestimate them yet, when sufficiently inspired, they can put men onto the moon in vessels made of tin foil. Look at the bold action that I was put up to in Chapter 3. Michael was waiting for my call. Gee was waiting for my call. Neither of them knew that they were waiting for my call, of course. They had no idea that I existed anymore than I had any clue that they existed but that is not the point here — although the Tiger will tell you that it is.

Whoever you need to speak with is waiting for your call, waiting to meet you. Turn it on its head for a moment. If somebody rang you up and stated that you were the person who could most help them, that you had the experience and wisdom to give them some advice and that they would like to travel across the country to visit you for some advice at a time of your choosing, would you say no?

So what's stopping you? The Tiger?

You can't find the number? Try harder. They say that there are only six degrees of separation, after all. Get on your email list, your social networking site, their website. Use your imagination and your creativity to work out how to get to them. If somebody offered you ten million pounds if you spoke to that person in the next twenty-four hours, would you be able to have a conversation with them then? Now there's a thought.

Have I got you back yet or are you still lost? Stay with me a little longer. We have to reach that killer question I promised.

There is one "but" in Rule 5

You may need to have established integrity with yourself (Rules 1–3) and be in control of yourself in pressure situations (Rule 4) before you'll make a real success of Rule 5. Let me explain with a story of something that happened in March 2008.

I was challenged hard on this Rule by a lady who worked for a British government body during a presentation after a gala dinner in Leeds.

"Hold on," she heckled, "Are you telling me that if I rang up Lord Andrew Lloyd Webber and asked him for a part in one of his musicals that he would give me one?"

"She's one hell of an amateur actress," her neighbour added.

"I don't know," I busked, "but I'll bet you a pound that if you call him up and say that you are prepared to do whatever it takes to be a musical theatre performer, that you've spent twelve months working and working at it in every spare minute of your time and then asked if he would give you ten minutes of advice, that he'd give you it."

She didn't accept the challenge. I guess she wasn't prepared to do anything at all. I think she wanted to publicly knock Rule 5 because it just might work — and that would require her to confront that she would never face up to the

Tiger of picking up the telephone or working with the tough Integrity Rules 1–4. Time to examine the 'X Factor Problem'.

The 'Reality TV Problem'

Rule 5 is a Leadership Rule. And the Leadership Rules enable you to take control of your story. Their foundations are the Integrity Rules, the courage to take bold actions, the willingness to question the Rulebook (all of that received wisdom that imprisons us), the courage to build a plan and every day, whatever happens, to put one foot in front of the other to hit our self-imposed deadlines.

People who think that Rule 5 can exist without Rules 1–4 are suffering from the 'Reality TV Problem' — the belief that it can be possible without the graft, just the luck. A belief backed up in our instant culture and by claims from self help 'gurus' that they can "make us happy/rich/thin" or that we can "manifest our destinies" with their help.

This is dangerous on three levels. On the one level, it is so preposterous that some people, knowing that this is hokum, become discouraged from trying any route. On a second level, it is dangerous because somebody who is not a 'natural' feels that it is unlikely that they will be plucked from obscurity by some god of their chosen profession and therefore lowers their sights. And on a third level, some of our youngsters are becoming discouraged from grafting to reach their goal and, instead, are sitting back, awaiting 'fame'.

Rule 5 says: Get yourself onto a reality TV show if you want to perform. Use any possible legal and ethical route to get there. But do not go on the television unless you have put in the graft to justify being there. Use it as a Rule 5 'tool' by all means, but not as a substitute for graft — unless you want to be mocked on prime time television, of course.

Now I said at the outset that the Rules do not need to be followed in order and they don't. You don't have to have established complete integrity of action before using Rule 5. You could, of course, use Rule 5 to get the advice necessary to decide on your bold action (Rule 1) or to gain a new perspective on your Rulebook (Rule 2). But do you see how they all begin to work together? How Rule 5 is not a shortcut? And that Rule 5 is a very, very powerful tool?

* * * * *

How do you hold a racehorse?

I'm still not sure I know the answer. But I'll take some small comfort from the fact that nobody seems to get it right one hundred percent of the time. But in early 2004 this was a burning question for me. Burning because if I didn't start getting better at it, I was going to lose the bet. Or worse, cause somebody an injury. Let me explain.

Shortly after Gee had introduced me to the Bosleys, she introduced me to their neighbour, Charlie Morlock. Charlie was another of the Kinsgton Lisle training community and he had also kindly agreed to give me a hand. Every day I would do two lots for the Bosleys, or two for Charlie, or carefully time a dash from one yard to the other to do one for each.

Another larger than life character who had ridden several winners over fences, Charlie soon welcomed me into the

Raceyard Cottage clan and was a huge help to me over the year. But, at first, his team weren't too impressed with the new addition. They had reason. I was making things a little more lively than things ought to be. I had also made no secret of my plan to ride on the track and I think they saw this Londoner who couldn't ride as just a bit cocky. A fair point.

During one of my first mornings at Charlie's, I was told to jump off (start cantering) at the back of the string and stay there. We were exercising the horses on the beautiful Blowing Stone Gallops in Kingston Lisle, which bends through almost ninety degrees around one third of the way up. The horses always try to speed up coming off of the bend and today was no exception. As we rounded the bend, my mount put his head down and went. I didn't hold him and we steamed through the string and past all of the others until I found myself trying to tuck him in behind the lead horse ridden by "Magic Hands" Leon. If I failed to hold him in behind Leon, nothing stood between me and a long white knuckle gallop across the Berkshire countryside.

The problem was that Leon, an experienced and very talented work rider in his late sixties, was sitting on one of the most difficult rides in the yard. And I had set it off. Leon's mount tried every trick to escape him but, incredibly, he was kept at a steady canter. I had a lot to learn.

We walked back to the yard quietly and untacked the horses. I was doing two lots today so there was breakfast in between and I wasn't really looking forward to it. I got into the kitchen at Raceyard Cottages before Leon and, not having ever met the man before, put my hand out to introduce myself. He shook my hand with the comment, "I think we've already met once this morning". Leon and I went on to become friends and he helped me a great deal with endless patient advice both alongside me on the gallops and on the way to and fro. But it was not a great start.

Shortly after that I was invited by Gee's fiancé, Mark Bradburne to visit Henry Daly's yard in Ludlow where he was stable jockey. As we approached the gallop after warming the horses up, Mark told me to stay eight lengths from him and to come no closer. There were only a couple behind me and the string of around fifteen horses was disappearing into the mist up the hill ahead. The sight was breathtaking and I felt great as we set off up the gallop.

I kept the mare eight lengths off Mark and was beginning to relax and enjoy the ride when I heard a shriek of "Look out — coming through!" — the shriek of a rider who is being runaway with and is warning you that they are about to set your horse alight as they pass. Off went the mare under me like a flash. I am now upsides Mark calling, "What do I do?" But I don't hear his answer as we disappear into the mist ahead of him. We weave through the string until, in the mist ahead, I begin to make out a dreadful sight — seven or eight of Mr Daly's finest chasers taking a turn at the top of the gallop. And a worse sight — Henry Daly in peaked cap and wellies standing beside his four wheel drive, watching the adventure unfold with a steely glare.

We are not slowing up. What happens now?

I decide to take action and steer the mare off of the gallop before we hit the others like so many hairy skittles. We head off into the mist on the field. Now gallops usually end at the top of hills and Mr Daly's was no exception. And if you gallop off of the top of a hill, you start to go down. And that means picking up speed. And we're off. Just the noise of

hooves and a horse breathing in the still, misty Ludow morning. And then we are joined by a third character. A fast-
approaching hedge. A huge hedge that I don't think she
could clear even if I had any idea how to jump over a hedge
on a horse. I'm really scared that I could hurt her if we don't
calm this down.

So I decide to bail out. Sit on the saddle, both feet out of
the irons, swing off, crunch.

I look up and the horse is at a calm trot leaving the field,
reins flapping and irons dangling through an unclosed gate.
I find that I can stand up ok. I look down and my front is covered in mud, head to toe. But otherwise I am fine.

I get back to the yard ten minutes later and the horse has
already been hosed down and is in her box. I decide to make
my peace with Mr Daly. At first he doesn't look like he is
ready to smoke a peace pipe with me. After a while we seem
to be okay again. Thank you Mr Daly. Sorry about that
Mark.

*Enough. Time for Rule 5, The Tools for Taming Tigers are
all around you.*

I did not want to ride out the next day. I didn't feel safe. It
wasn't about not 'getting back on the horse', it was about
damaging somebody or hurting a horse. So I didn't. I simply
didn't know how to do it and everybody told me it was 'feel'.
Well I didn't seem to have much 'feel' and I didn't have a lot
of time to get some either. I rang Gee and told her that I
wouldn't ride out until I could hold one better. That night,
Gee, Mark and I made a plan.

It may not seem radical to you, but it was pretty radical in
racing terms. We would borrow a racehorse that had not

been out exercising that day. We'd take it to a gallop after all of the other horses had gone home. And I would pull it up. And pull it up and pull it up and pull it up until I could pull it up every time.

Mark came along, Gee came along and Charlie — who had leant us a racehorse — came along too. I don't know what I ever did to deserve friends like these but Charlie was at the start of the gallop to help me start off steady and not get into a battle, Gee part way along to call advice about my position in the saddle and Mark varied his position beyond Gee to make different stopping points. We were not to pull up at the end of the gallop where the horse knew that pulling up was expected, but at *exactly* the point where Mark stood along the way.

I had Charlie, a former jockey and talented trainer, Gee, a former champion lady jockey and Mark, a top flight jump jockey who had just come second in the Grand National standing in a field teaching me to hold a horse. How did that happen?

Rule 5. People are great

After half an hour that confused our horse considerably — but that he seemed to enjoy — I was good. Not great. But I had a whole different approach and I was getting stronger in the saddle. I also had some confidence back. The Rule 5 "Tools" had included creativity, breaking some racing 'norms' and telling some great people that I badly needed their help. We were back on track and I would ride out again tomorrow.

The killer question

Of course, by now, you know the question and have probably been hoping that I would not ask it.

Why have you not put the book down and called the person in this world who could most help you to write the next chapter? Surely it's not the Tiger stopping you?

Over to you.

Case study: Paul Croft

I've never been to one of Jim's presentations but I receive his newsletter, it's one of a number of business gurus' mailing lists that I am on. I also undergo sports psychology too, to help with my golf, which I play regularly, taking part in competitions. As well as sport, I'm also interested in military history and would like to move in to doing that full-time one day.

"To succeed at golf, I found the best guys I could to work with and sought their coaching and advice. Making phone calls to strangers can lead to all kinds of opportunities you might never have expected."

My career has been a mixture of sales and consultancy jobs but I am first and foremost a salesman. I started out selling chewing gum in 1977. In 1996 when I was forty, I went to University to study Business. Some friends thought I was mad to try it at that age but I had a great experience and I've never regretted it. I'm now a client care consultant looking after my own department.

I became interested in self-development after going to see a speaker in the early 1980s. Throughout the 1980s I continued my interest, going on Chartered Institute of Marketing sales management courses. Of Jim's Ten Rules for Taming Tigers, the ones I identify with most are: 'There is no safety in numbers', as people have a habit of letting you down; 'Do something scary every day', and 'Never, never give up'.

The Tiger I have been working on taming is my temperament. I believe in fairness to the point of bombast and can be a bit 'in your face'. I'm quite a 'type A' personality and have trouble dealing with people who aren't as driven as me.

Sports and in particular, golf, has always been a major driver for me and is one instance in which I apply the Rules. I have been playing golf for thirty years but I became serious when I was at university as I had more time to play. Recently, I have had some major successes, including coming second in the President's Cup at my golf club earlier this year, achieving a personal best.

To succeed at golf, I found the best guys I could to work with and sought their coaching and advice, as Jim's fifth Rule says, 'the tools for Taming Tigers are all around you'. Making phone calls to strangers can lead to all kinds of opportunities you might never have expected. My golfing successes have affected other areas of my life. I'm now more timing and appointment-driven. The more I keep to my appointments, the more time I have to play golf! I have a plan and a direction I'm moving towards, but it's adaptable and changes as I need it to.

Last year I had Tigers to tame in my personal life after my wife was diagnosed with breast cancer. It's been a difficult time and I have been really working on focus.

A few years ago I was in a car accident where I was hit by a lorry at seventy miles per hour. It took me a long time to recover and it made me feel like giving up, but I pulled through it. Because of these experiences I feel I understand the importance of never, ever giving up. You only get one crack at life so you have to look after yourself.

Chapter 9

Rule 6: There is no safety in numbers

Where would you go to find the most brilliant jockeys in the world?

When I ask this from the stage the most common response is Ireland. The most unusual is Mongolia. I must go there someday soon and see for myself!

In my experience, if you want to find the most brilliant jockeys — the ones who *really* understand race tactics, who *really* know how to judge a gap, who *really* know how to read a race unfolding around them, and who know *exactly* how a particular animal will respond to a given request from the rider — you go to the racetrack bar or the press room.

In the bar, you will find the gentleman who is five or six stones too heavy to race and, incidentally, has never sat on a riding school pony, never mind a racehorse in training at 6am on the roads of Lambourn or Newmarket. Early mornings and the risk of a fall are not really his cup of tea. He's nursing his third beer of the day at 3pm and he's watching the racing on the bar's television because it's cold out there by the track — and it looks like rain.

In the press room, salaried writers make or break reputations based on their assessment of what has unfolded on the track. Many will broadcast their assumptions and work squarely within their own unchallenged Rulebooks whilst passing judgments, making kings and publicly allocating blame. Only a select few have ridden in races. They are always worth reading.

Where, on your metaphorical racecourse do you wish to be, my friend? In the bar? In the press room?

Or on the track?

Surely all of the people that we admire have spent their lives avoiding the temptation to sit down too long in the grandstand. They all preferred to be on the track. Or, if not 'preferred', they knew that that was where they would *have* to place themselves in order to write their own story to their own satisfaction.

Whilst the others watched and passed judgment, our heroes became accustomed to how exposed they felt as they cantered past the grandstand to post on their big day. That's a lot of people over there, and a lot of cameras. There is nowhere to hide from their judgment out on the track.

Leaving the stalls, they're concentrating on perfect balance and finding the perfect position for their horse rather than on the danger that they are suddenly launched into. They have their breath taken away by the speed of acceleration and the pace of the race, by how fast it happens out there, but they concentrate on keeping a steady breath; trying to perform everything that they have practiced under the pressure of the race.

Surely and steadily they round the home straight to see the grandstand and the winning post ahead. They suddenly hit the noise of the commentator barking out onto the track as they get lower in the saddle and begin to work hard with their horse to produce one last surge of effort. They keep an eye to each side as other horses begin to challenge them and the race gets serious — maybe three, maybe four in a row now — horses eyeball to eyeball, competing hard with each other. They ask the horse for more and watch it compete with the horse next to it — competing hard and loving it — jockeys clanking stirrups at thirty-seven miles per hour, horses barging. Gaps opening — or closing — and all the time, the line approaching.

They meet the wall of sound — the roar of the crowd — and as soon as they meet it, it's gone. Distant and behind them, as they calm the horse and bring it to a gentle canter, then a trot. Then turn to leave the track. Elated? Ecstatic? Years of dieting, exercising, learning, committing, falling off and getting back on, winning allies and supporters finally bringing the prize.

Or disappointment. Maybe even devastation. Maybe a feeling of having let great supporters down, of having missed a moment that, with wondrous hindsight, was theirs for the taking. A decision that was taken in the rush of competition that may have been the wrong call. The video watching. The analysing. The slow recovery. The self criticism in the dead of night.

Our friends in the warm of the grandstand know little of this process, but they'd be quick to pass judgment if they lost a few pounds on the race.

And yes, indeed, our press friends' words are exposing. They publish them, after all. They open themselves to criticism, but they have the editor, the sounding boards, the luxury of time in arriving at a decision. A young jockey goes out onto the track with nobody to help him or her avoid making mistakes. Without a pint to make them brave as they hold forth. No place to hide.

All of our heroes were on the track, making things happen.

And you cannot tame your Tiger from the grandstand.

For you, sir or madam, this may be old news. You have been out there trying your best, exposed, for years and you know the feeling well. They have criticised you and you have withstood the barbs. Perhaps you have pushed through that phase and perhaps they have even eaten their words.

But maybe that is not you. Maybe you, in company with most humans, prefer the crowd. The grandstand. Spectating others' adventures. Judging the performance of others. Watching as they write the story of their lives. As they make things happen.

Rule 6 of the Ten Rules for Taming Tigers is this:

There is no safety in numbers.

Our media will tell us that there is. Our families often tell us that there is. Our schools almost always tell us that there is (whilst we are there and also in their advice to us about the great adventure that awaits us). And we often persuade ourselves that there is. It is so much more appealing than facing the Tiger's attempts to scare us away from the exposing track.

So, why, when it is clear to a child that the real adventures are not to be had whilst we run like a wildebeest with the herd, do we persist in sticking with the crowd?

The Tiger tells us to.

Now let me make an important distinction. I don't believe that any aspect of Tiger taming requires us to run against the crowd for the sake of it. This is not about being rebellious for no reason. I don't believe that any part of Tiger taming involves ignoring good solutions that others have already created when we could (ethically) borrow or build upon their work. Neither is Rule 6 about arrogantly ignoring the advice or feedback of others whose assistance we would be wise to accept.

No. Rule 6 is about not fearing to stand up and be counted when the time comes — even if that means that they'll be talking about you in the stands, wherever the stands are in your world. Rule 6 is about not fearing to be judged by others, thought foolish or 'above oneself' when the time comes to make your move, to stand up and be counted, to make things happen. On the track, we have to cash the cheques that our mouths write. On the track, there is nowhere to hide and no excuses.

Spotting oneself in the grandstand

Whenever you find yourself passing judgment on others, in your head or in company, take a pause. Are you becoming a 'grandstand jockey'? It is fun, for sure. It spreads negativity and fear around our societies, for sure. It inhibits innovation and crushes youth, for sure. But, above all, it makes us feel good. A reassuring feeling of belonging to a group. A group that knows best. Although almost certainly none of the group has been on the track.

One very interesting thing that I noticed when I began to meet professional sportspeople is how little 'grandstand jockeying' they do. How impressed and pleased they are by achievement in any field, because they know the price of achievement. How generous they are in their congratulations. How they tend to empathise with somebody who has made a bad decision, because they know the self-criticism and anguish that comes from a bad call made with only the very best of intentions.

They share a humility that prevents them from judging and that perhaps can only come from realising how close one is, personally, at any moment, to the humiliation that comes from putting oneself to the test, way outside of the safety zone, in a public forum.

So any Tiger tamer needs to develop an awareness of when they are straying into the grandstand to join the quagmire of judgment that confronts those, at any level of society, who are attempting to make something happen. Finding oneself in the grandstand is a sure sign that you are not on the track. It is hard to be in two places at once.

Leaving the grandstand

When we can see the world and the Rulebook that society wants us to live by for what it is — rather than from the inside looking out — then we can choose to go onto the track and look back at all the faces in the grandstand.

For anybody who is out on the track, loneliness comes and loneliness goes. Harsh self-criticism comes with the turf. If you take the decision not to run with the pack, the pack will want to feed on you from time to time, and sometimes you'll find yourself wondering if they are right after all.

But if you take the decision not to run with the pack, perhaps you will meet other Tiger tamers. You will run with a new crowd. You will gain new supporters and admirers. And these are people who will take your call late at night when you are smarting, because they have been stung too.

And then there is the thrill when you get it right. When you know you took the decision and backed it with your reputation and lost sleep about it and cared.

And you made it happen.

And you won.

Case study: Katrina Dunkley

I've known and worked with Jim for many years as one of his customers during my time in a major blue chip company. Jim has a
fantastic record in improving communications and presentation
skills so I've purposefully kept in touch with him.

"My work Tiger was a fear of failure on my own. Following careful prepara-tion, I left work 3 months after returning from my Himalayan adventure. I started freelancing."

A couple of years ago we met for a catch up and he shared with me his plan to write a book, Ten Rules for Taming Tigers. He explained his vision and what it was he meant by 'Tigers' and I was totally wowed. Jim also talked about his ambition to become a jockey and I was really inspired by his motivation and determination. We agreed to set chal-lenges for each other. Jim committed to both his book and his riding and he challenged me to achieve some personal dreams too.

My partner of seventeen years is a very keen motorcyclist. I'd
passed my bike test years ago but had always taken the easier and
safer ride and sat on the back. After meeting up with Jim, I
realised how much I wanted to ride myself and travel somewhere
unusual and exciting with my chap, so this was the Tiger I agreed
with Jim I wanted to tame.

I thought long and hard about my exciting and adventurous
destination and eventually settled on the Himalayas, on roads and
tracks that take you all the way to the Tibetan border. Once the
trip was booked, I knew there was no turning back!

In order to succeed, I knew I needed to make a plan. I started
my preparations by doing a refresher course as it had been years
since I'd ridden. I then took a two day 'off-roading' course, led by

the coach who trained Ewan McGregor and Charlie Boorman for their epic bike trip, *The Long Way Round*. It wasn't easy, I constantly fell off, the bike was enormous and lifting it was seriously hard work and tiring. My Tiger bit back continuously! I felt frustrated that I would never be competent enough to complete the challenge of riding in India where the roads in most places are no more than rubble tracks. Knowing that I'd already booked and paid for the holiday was a massive incentive to keep focused and motivated to succeed.

On arrival in India, we went to Shimla, where we hired Royal Enfield motorbikes and set off on our trip. It was the most amazing experience I have ever had. We rode approximately one thousand kilometres in awful conditions. The monsoons had swept what little roads there were away and it was treacherous for most of the way. I fell off every day. The waterfall crossings were the worst, but I just kept on going, absolutely determined to complete under my own steam. I tamed my Tiger and now I ride everywhere. Next year I'm planning to ride across America from East to West Coast.

But I had, and still have other Tigers to tame. In my professional life, I have only ever worked for one company, for twenty-nine years. For a number of years I had a growing ambition to work for myself but lacked the confidence to make the break. My employer was my home and my family and to leave felt like I'd be stepping off a cliff — seriously scary stuff. I knew that if I was to succeed I'd need to build a bridge from my old life to a new world; otherwise I'd be just walking the plank!

After my Indian adventure, I became more convinced that I could leave and make it on my own. My plan was to freelance as a learning and development specialist, focussing on the areas of leadership, change management, and performance management. Jim's Rules for Taming Tigers gave me the motivation to start building my bridge. What I find really inspiring about Jim is that he really practises what he preaches. He responded to an audience challenge to become a jockey, and this has given him massive credibility. As a person, his enthusiasm is motivational and inspirational and a driving force for two major personal achievements in one year.

My work Tiger was a fear of failure on my own. Following careful preparation, I left work three months after returning from my Himalayan adventure. I started freelancing in January 2008. My preparation was building my bridge and I have safely and successfully crossed. I worked hard to gather and exploit considerable support from those around me and had to convince my partner I'd be able to succeed commercially on my own. To date, I haven't had any big setbacks in my new business yet but it's important to say that's because I've applied the skills acquired in my twenty-nine year career and this has helped to mitigate my risks to date. Sheer determination, 'will' as Jim puts it, has been the primary motivator however and driven me on to overcome obstacles as they occur.

My business is going well so far. I have a great work-life balance now and the opportunity to plan lots more Himalayan-type trips! But Taming Tigers is an ongoing process and I have other Tigers to tame — my next challenge is public speaking, so forever onwards!

[Editor's note: As we went to press, Katrina had accepted an engagement to speak to 160 people at a sales conference at London's Olympia]

Part Four

The Change Rules

Chapter 10

Rule 7: Do something scary everyday

Now, you may well have spotted by now that this is a book about risk and dealing with our reaction to risk. Our reaction to risk is, often, fear.

No. There isn't really a Tiger. It would be a very different book if there were. However real and noisy the Tiger may be, he isn't *really* there, is he? There's just us, trying our best to get it right out there; assessing risks and getting scared about taking them when the status quo seems acceptable.

In many decisions that we take, we weigh up the desired outcome versus the risk of action. "I want that cake, but I fear there may soon be just a little too much of me for my liking." Or, "I want to speak with that stranger but I fear they may think that I am dull." Or, "I want to tell my boss my great idea and put some passion and commitment into this discussion but I fear they may reject me so I shall let them take the decisions and advise from the grandstand after the meeting".

We could go on. The point of this book is to underscore the risk and consequence of *inaction* and to attempt to provide assistance in dealing with the risks and fear involved in taking action.

Where we are today is the sum of all of those decisions that we have taken over the years. Tomorrow we shall add on the consequences of the decisions that we take today. Sure, the environment we operate in may influence how we approach those decisions. The habits of thought that were or are prevalent in our homes (parents or spouses, for example) may be infectious. We may even choose to blame those who share these habits, or those who demonstrated them to us, for their detrimental effects upon our lives, but, once we have that out of our systems, perhaps we have to recognise the strong likelihood that we are the ones responsible. We make the decisions. We get the results.

So, if we are the sum of our decisions, and our decisions are influenced by our attitude to risk, then the way that we perceive and react to risk will play a huge part in the results that we get in our lives. Our attitude to and appetite for risk is, perhaps, the defining factor in the results that we achieve, in our ability to write the story that we want to write, rather than having to accept the story that the Tiger has dictated to us.

Rule 7 is not about thrill seeking, although you could use thrills to help you become more comfortable with risk. Rule 7 is not about acting rashly, recklessly, negligently or without regard for others.

Rule 7 is about flexing the 'risk muscle', daily in a controlled environment of our choosing and in a considered fashion. Rule 7 is about becoming a little more daring, every day. Rule 7 is about coping with Rule 6 and moving away from the crowd, facing the isolation that may be necessary to make your stand, so that you can dare to imagine and then to dare to create (Rule 3). Rule 7 is about laying down challenges to your Rulebook (Rule 2) and even about taking bold actions today (Rule 1) rather than thinking things over for another year or ten.

The Change Rules

Rule 7 is also the first of the Change Rules. As we examined together in Chapter 4, the Change Rules are about consolidating our gains and becoming consistent in Taming our Tigers. Without these Rules, we have achievements rather than progress. We might achieve something interesting but we are not moving consistently onto that higher level — consolidating the gains, making it permanent.

So in the Change Rules we look at the roles that getting into the habit of taking risks (Rule 7), building a different relationship with time (Rule 8) and putting new personal disciplines in place (Rule 9) can achieve in Taming Tigers in both the short and long term.

So let's look at the Tiger Cycle and how to break out of it and create change. Have a look at Figure 1.

A challenge of some kind hits us — "Deliver a presentation to a group of twenty people!" — and we immediately begin assessing the risk that this challenge poses to us in the light of our Rulebook (Rule 2). Let's suppose that we have a rule that says, "I am a bad presenter. I know this because I have received feedback to tell me that I am a bad presenter. In fact, seeing as we live in the twenty-first century, the age

Breaking the Tiger Cycle.

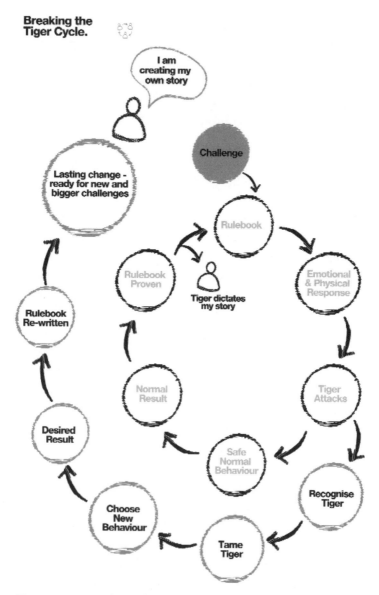

Figure 1 — Breaking the Tiger Cycle

of 360 degree feedback, everybody has been telling me that I am a bad presenter."

By this stage, you are probably having a response. It is emotional and it will also be physical. It is being caused by the interaction of the challenge and your personal Rulebook. It bears no relation to reality, of course, because the Rulebook is an entirely fictional thing, designed to keep us safe (see Rule 2). That's not to say that you are not, in reality, a bad presenter. You may be abysmal, for all I know — I've never seen you present. But that is something that you can change in a day if you want to change it. Anybody can. The idea that it is a 'rule' that you are a bad presenter — that's the fiction.

Assuming for a moment that we find the risk too unpleasant to contemplate, we could choose to engage our intellect to alter the Rulebook. We could choose to seek training, to prepare with the assistance of a colleague who is an excellent presenter. We could choose to rehearse in the evenings in front of the family camcorder until we feel that we are doing an excellent job. But most people do not choose to engage their intellect. They permit their emotional response to override their desire to do a good job.

They are meeting the Tiger and permitting it to write their story.

We have options here. We can stick to safe, normal behaviour and deliver our usual poor presentation. And we will almost certainly get our usual poor response. We will have our Rulebook well and truly reinforced by the experience ("I *am* a bad presenter — just look at their faces! Poor me, why was I born without this module fitted correctly?") and we will probably dread the next invitation to present. The Tiger Cycle continues.

We are choosing to permit the Tiger to dictate the next chapter of our story — the chapter where we could write about grabbing a great opportunity to raise our profile, to create some energy and passion around ourselves, our team and our ideas through a presentation. We choose to let the Tiger write a different chapter for us. A chapter where we stand at the side of the room and speak in a monotone to a projector or screen. A chapter where people think that the idea was a bit weak and that the person who presented it has very probably met their career limits.

But we kept ourselves safe from the fear of taking a risk and changing stuff. What we missed, of course, was the risk inherent in doing it the way we always had — the damage to the story that we could have been writing. The damage to the people in our team.

Breaking the Tiger Cycle

In the Taming Tigers philosophy, we begin to create real change when we begin to recognise the Tiger — the thing that we have constructed to roar at us at any point when we face a change that causes us concern — is a luxury that we are no longer content to indulge in. We have a story to write, a duty to friends, family, colleagues and ourselves. So it has to be tamed. It has to be faced.

By facing the Tiger down rather than reacting to it, we move onto the outer path in Figure 1. Suddenly, we recognise that the emotional and physical responses, real though they are, are brought about by the interaction of the challenge and the Rulebook. And guess what? We are in charge of the Rulebook! So now, using the Ten Rules, we *can* get past the Tiger, we *can* choose new behaviours and we *can* get the result that we desire. And that new result will impact on the Rulebook, won't it? "I *can* present! Look at me! Bring it on!"

And now we have a change.

Why does change cause us concern?

Why would a change cause concern? Simple. When we weigh up whether or not to make a change, we face uncertainty. And nothing causes a human being concern like uncertainty. *Isn't that true, drinkers? Would we be funny? Would we ever get off to sleep again?* We may also face a period of readjustment. And we don't like the thought of that much either, *do we smokers?*

And the big one, the main concern if we are actually think about a major change? We might fail. *And that would never do, would it grumbling job-haters who won't risk a change of job? Better the devil you know, eh?*

But we rarely apply Rule 8 to the proceedings. We rarely recognise the fact that the long term certainty, the result that we are sure to achieve if we continue to invest our time, day after day, in avoiding this Tiger, is far more scary: The illness and the ruined relationships of the addict, or the bitterness and victim-vibe that surrounds the long-term job-hater.

Why does change so often fail?

I have never subscribed to the theory that people are 'barriers' to change. I believe that the Tiger is. And I think that our duty, if we wish to change ourselves or to assist others to change — for example, leading change in the workplace or helping our children through adolescence — is to work in the area of the Tiger in preference to 'carrot and sticking' people into the new way of doing things. Integrity and leadership will be the foundations of this work, followed by consolidating the change and making 'the new' into 'the norm', and finally the growth of individual and/or group esteem, growing confidence in themselves and in the new way of doing things. And there we have the four sections of this book.

I think that this is exactly the same whether we are dealing with a large corporate change programme or asking ourselves to make a change, such as to stop overeating or to make time to spend with the kids. It is about asking human beings to do things differently. So when we ask people to change, including a request to ourselves, we focus on what to do differently, how and by when. The 1st January style list of 'resolutions'. And, in my experience, people try hard to work with that.

Let's keep it simple. Think of it in a training course. We are told that we will do better if we act in a new way, 'exhibit certain new behaviours'. These new behaviours are alien to us and when we are asked to perform them under pressure, they cause the Tiger to run from cover right into our path and roar! So over time, so painful are the new behaviours to us, we revert to the old ways. Who would blame us? I have demonstrated this in Figure 2.

And that is how Taming Tigers came to have life — in the worlds of cultural change and of training. If we can tackle the Tiger, we can create new and exciting possibilities for

The Traditional Training Cycle.

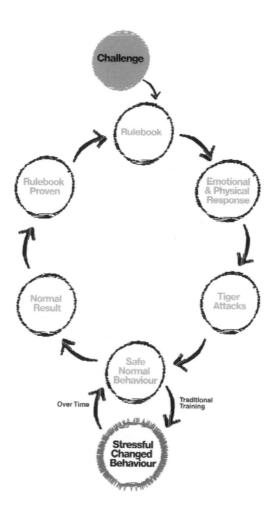

Figure 2 — The Traditional Training Cycle.

people. Or rather — they can create them for themselves. Now we're writing a story!

And if we do that, how do we keep the momentum going and make the change a habit?

Rule 7 is this:

Do something scary every day

So if the whole of this book is about understanding our perception of risk and the way we react to the fear that we feel as a result, how can Rule 7 assist us?

Rule 7 assists us in a number of different ways:

- It keeps us aware of the Tiger. We can't let it lurk around the perimeter of our experiences to date, roaring at them if they try to expand. We know him now. We listen to him roar every day when we do a scary thing and we realise he has no teeth. We lived!
- It creates the energy and excitement to do something every day that causes a release of adrenaline into the system, builds your confidence and makes the 'rut' a thing of the past.
- It builds learning, progress, and advancement into the day. When we take a risk, we learn something. Always. If we are doing that in a controlled and careful way — creating and planning opportunities for ourselves every day — then we are on an impressive personal growth trajectory. We are also building a new relationship with time, examining the Rulebook. We are learning about the Tiger. We are learning about risk.

This continued growth effect through being just a little outside of the safety zone every day was the most important factor in allowing me to get to the racetrack at the pace that I did. Gee managed it brilliantly too — always presenting a new challenge about a month sooner than I would have volunteered for it.

Rule 7 at the races — a Tiger Tamer well outside his safety zone

It's 23rd December 2003, my thirty-sixth birthday. It is 5.45am, pitch black and the frost on the verges is sparkling in my headlights. I have driven down from London, I'm in the backstreets of Upper Lambourn and I am hopelessly lost.

I'm not very good at being late — it's a personal thing, it makes me stressed. The fact that I'm visiting Jamie Osborne's famous yard for the first time, won't know anybody when I arrive there, and will have to sit on a horse in front of all of those experienced riders is not making me feel better about the situation. I have been riding for one month and one day. Gee has set this up for me, but even she's not daft enough to be up at this hour to watch me try to ride a horse.

I turn a corner to see a sight that I have never seen before — a string of fifteen racehorses, all ridden by riders wearing luminous yellow tabards, is coming down the road towards me in the dark. I'll never forget the first time I heard that mass clacking of hooves on tarmac. For some reason, it is still a sound that makes me feel really good whenever I hear it. As I wind down my window to ask for directions it dawns on me that they're not going to stop the string to speak to me, so I try to call out to a rider three of four down the string in the hope that he or she can answer by the time they've got past. I get some muffled directions and it turns out that I'm pretty close to Osborne's yard. I put the handbrake on in the car park at 6.05am. This is a bad, bad introduction. Racing yards don't do late.

But my problems haven't even begun. I'm now lost in a massive yard, trying to find the one person who is expecting me, Jamie's Assistant Trainer, Roddy Llewelyn. In around half of the boxes there is a light on and a body working away inside. Ominously, there is also a fully tacked up horse in each box ready to pull out as soon as the cry "pull out" goes up. I haven't even found my bridle and at this stage, I'm not tacking up at speed. I eventually find Roddy, who doesn't look impressed that I'm late, but immediately senses that I'm a bit on edge and is good enough to put me at ease with a smile and a handshake.

"You're riding Jamie's cob, Victor, today."

"Great, thanks."

"He's easier than a racehorse, but he's a bit of a stubborn so and so with an attitude. He likes to take the piss. Do you reckon you can handle that?"

Oh, Gee! What have you set me up for here? My heart starts pounding and I do my best to reply with a cheery "we'll be fine" to Roddy. Roddy's also beginning to look as if he's wondering what Gee has set him up for.

"Pull out!" Riders are being legged up and the string starts to move towards the covered trotting track to warm their horses up. Roddy and I approach Victor's box. Roddy's carrying the tack and, thank all the saints and angels and everybody else, immediately sets about tacking Victor up rather than leaving it to me.

He leads Victor out of the box, legs me up and tells me to check my girth (the strap that holds the saddle in place).

Check my girth? Whilst I'm actually sitting on the horse? Little do I know that it's perfectly normal for work riders to be tightening and loosening their girth at different stages of the morning whilst they sit in the saddle. This seems like an impossible feat to me at this stage. I look at Roddy in alarm. He looks back at me, slightly more alarmed.

He tightens the girth and tells me to trot round the trotting school with the others. He jogs on ahead to get into the school and start giving the riders their instructions.

We go through the dark, frosty morning towards the lit trotting area. It's like a big sandy running track with a fence at either side. It's smaller in circumference than a running track and probably only a third as wide. The track itself is covered with a pitched roof and there are lights in the roof so that we can see what we're doing. The centre is uncovered, just an area of grass that doesn't seem to have a use. As I get closer, I can see around twenty five racehorses moving round at a brisk trot. This is the first time I've seen anything like this. This is the first time, other than on the street just now, that I've seen work riders let alone racehorses. I am amazed at how casual they all seem, and how relaxed they are in their work. I thought this was meant to be dangerous! Maybe it's all going to be okay. Some are standing up in their irons others rising in their trot, some are speaking to each other and others are riding around on their own or talking to their horses. All are so wrapped up with balaclavas, scarves, gloves and numerous layers underneath their jackets that they look like little footballs sitting on top of their horses.

In I go and kick Victor into a trot — except he doesn't trot. Now don't get me wrong, it's not that he won't go — he certainly isn't walking — unbeknownst to me he has understood, from the moment that I entered the box, that I know nothing about how to deal with the wily character he prides himself on being, and as soon as he sees that he's out with the big boys, he wants to prove himself. So he moves from walk to canter in a blink, and we're off, weaving our way between the work riders who are not slow to yell their disapproval back at me as I set their horses alight by carving through them.

Except that I'm not the one carving through them, I'm not steering this thing at all, Victor is in charge. I ease back to start pulling against his mouth and realise that my reins are far too long — I hadn't been ready for the canter — so I quickly change my hands to shorten up the reins. Now this, I will learn in weeks to come, is a sign for thoroughbreds to speed up. If you watch jockeys approaching the finishing line at a race, you'll always see them shortening their reins and changing hands. It's like pressing down on the throttle of a racehorse.

You might think it wouldn't be the same for a cob, but it turns out that Victor's been hanging around racehorses for far too long and he takes a change of hands as a very clear signal to speed up. Up until now I merely felt total embarrassment. These experienced riders seem to be able to sit on their jumpy three and four year olds, even with Victor and I cantering steadily through them, so I'm not too afraid at this stage. But the burst of speed that this little cob gives me as I change my hands ups the stakes considerably. Now I'm worried.

I'm now getting some very 'straightforward' advice from each rider as I pass them. But for me, for some reason, sitting up here totally powerless, I suddenly start to notice how loud the wind is going past my ears. There's really not much else that I can notice up here. I can't stop this horse, and the view that I'm getting is a little bit like the view you get on a computer game, sitting in a car that's dodging and weaving its way past other cars at a rate of knots on the track, leaving havoc in its wake. I am awake, having a nightmare.

I'm on my third lap now. I've lapped most of the horses in here at least twice and, as I come round, Roddy decides that action needs to be taken. He's standing in the middle of the school with his arms outstretched — is he mad? He stares Victor straight in the eye. And Victor stares at him back. And I stare from one to the other and wonder what's going to happen to us all next.

Victor is clearly a sports fan. Not only has he been hanging out with the racehorses, but he knows how to sell a dummy. He jinks left, but Roddy's no fool and he leaps over to the outside of the track in front of Victor. Victor picks up speed and, as he gets to Roddy, he jinks right. He's beaten that last defender and there's nothing between him and the line. His ears prick and he steadily enjoys his moment of victory.

Victor can think of no more fun to have. He's outrun every racehorse that is exercising in first lot and his cocky pricked ears are asking the trotting thoroughbreds, "who's the daddy?" But better, he's put in a sidestep that would have made Phil Bennett proud. He pulls himself up to a trot, sticks in a great victory buck, dumps me on the ground and trots round to where Roddy is waiting to pick him up. I walk back around the track to meet up with Roddy and the enemy.

Sometimes it's the little things in Tiger Taming that seem hard, like having a whole string of riders look at you in disgust! One girl smiled at me on that walk to Roddy. Thanks, Sam.

Roddy's a total gent and tries really hard to smile and tell me not to worry about it. As we walk back to the box whilst the rest of the string meanders their way on to the all-weather gallop for their morning canter, Roddy asks if I wouldn't mind being on time tomorrow morning.

Oh, god. Only twenty-three hours left until I have to do this 'scary thing' again. And again.

Until eventually it is the 23rd October 2004 and there is just under a month to go until we race. I jump in the car at my new home in East Garston and drive the fifteen minutes to Charlie Morlock's. It's a crisp day and it's exciting. There's another scary thing to do today. I'm doing my first piece of work on Airgusta, whom I'll be riding in my race. I've exercised him before but not worked him.

It's a Saturday morning but the yard is buzzing with activity when I arrive and there's great banter as we all check who is riding what on the notice board in the tack room, gather up the tack and head off to the boxes. Ten minutes later, we're pulling out into Kingston Lisle. The Blowing Stone gallop is ahead, winding up the hill, looking great in the sun. But we're not going there. We're working on a flat all-weather gallop where they can really get some speed up.

We pass Martin and Sarah Bosley's string warming up at a trot through the village. They slow to a walk to pass us and once we're all past and the "hellos" are done, we trot on down to the gallop. We jump off and take a steady canter from one end of the gallop to the other. And with this and the trot, Charlie is happy that the horses are ready to do their fast work. We walk back to the start.

I've ridden work for Charlie and for Bos and I've worked at it at the British Racing School in Newmarket, but I still have to think things through beforehand so that I don't miss anything. The first time that you ride work is breathtaking. The speed that you reach is, because it is on a horse and not a machine, like nothing that you have experienced before and you are so close to each other that at first you can't believe it'll work out. But it does.

Charlie gives me and Leon our instructions. Leon is to jump off first, I am to be tight behind, go on a good clip before joining at the second bush and letting them go on a stride, upsides for the rest of the gallop. Okay. Goggles down, girth re-checked. The horses are on their toes — they know exactly what's coming and they couldn't be more excited.

Leon jumps off and I am tight in behind. Airgusta shakes his head at me and pulls to go and race but he comes back to me and quickly settles. We're belting along now, trees blurring to the right, grass to the left and the noise of hooves and wind. He's giving me a great feel — well-oiled movement and nicely balanced — it'll be great to go racing with him. He's also facing a lot of kickback here — sand being thrown up by the hooves of the horse in front. He'll have to deal with the same at Southwell and he doesn't seem to even notice it's there.

First bush. I pull him out from behind Leon, trying to anticipate the tug that will come as he takes our move to be a signal to speed up. He's a racehorse and he knows his job. I want the speed, but only enough to join Leon at the second bush — then we'll go on together. If he gets too much speed on now, we'll fly past Leon and the work is totally wrecked.

He comes back to me again but only just. I'm swinging off the back of him now as we get to Leon. I need to be toe to toe with Leon, boots touching before we accelerate together. Then we stay together. Working to the weaker horse — nobody 'wins' this piece of work.

Leon grins over as my iron clanks against his precisely as we arrive at the second bush — he's helped so much to get me here.

"Ready?" he yells above the thunder.

"Ready!"

A gentle easing forward of weight, a fraction more rein and he flies! We're stride for stride for a furlong until he feels like he's about to weaken. Click in the back of my mouth, Change hands, drop lower in the saddle and he's back.

We flash past Charlie and I just manage to glimpse that he's grinning. Airgusta is doing really well.

"Okay!" Leon calls. We both lengthen the reins and stand up in the saddles a little with a "Whoa!" and they slow up and trot into the turning circle at the end.

"That'll do. Take 'em home" Charlie yells to us. And Leon and I start the journey back through Kingston Lisle to Raceyard Cottages.

Whoever would have thought when I wrote "Do something scary everyday" into that first speech that it would lead me to this?

Case study: Chris Pierce

I saw Jim speak at the itSMF (IT Service Management Forum) conference for IT service management professionals in Birmingham in November 2006. I enjoy conference presentations but in the past,

> *"Do something scary every day is a good principle and I still try to do it, even if it's something quite small. It's not just my professional life where things have changed, I've started doing things I'd been putting off in other areas of my life."*

I've been frustrated by speakers who don't use plain language or give practical tips. With Jim I was impressed by what I saw straight away, in particular his idea about doing something scary every day. In fact, I was so inspired that I decided there and then to speak at the following year's conference. I mentioned it to the colleague who was with me and she didn't believe that I would see it through. I assured her that I would — even though it would be the scariest thing I'd ever done — and that she was my witness!

I have worked in IT for the Police for nearly thirty years and if I'm honest, I had become used to being in my comfort zone, so this was a big thing to put myself forward for. The first step was submitting a synopsis for my presentation. I called my talk *Think of it like this . . .! (The power of analogies and doughnuts in getting your message across)*. I was determined it would be interesting and it wouldn't be 'death by PowerPoint'. At this stage, I wasn't looking forward to presenting and was wondering why I had put myself forward for it — the Tiger I had set out to tame was biting back. Once I had heard that my application had been accepted, I knew I had to go through with it. I was to speak at the November 2007 conference in Brighton.

When it came to the conference, I wasn't sure how much interest there would be in my presentation but there turned out to be a full house — there were even people standing lining the sides of the room! I started by saying that this was one of the biggest day of my life, and that I wouldn't have been there without Jim and several people in the room, who had also seen Jim speak, nodded.

The talk itself went fantastically well and there were laughs and cheers in all the right places. In the conference feedback statistics I received afterwards, ninety-five percent of those who attended said that the presentation was very good or excellent and one hundred percent said they would recommend me as a speaker for future events.

I would go so far as to say that Jim has changed my life, as if it hadn't been for his keynote presentation, I would never have gone on to present myself. I've carried on presenting and I'm now on the itSMF list of speakers. I recently wrote an editorial for Computer Weekly magazine too. I now have a different outlook and want to inspire others to do the same myself. I carry the card with the Ten Rules for Taming Tigers in my pocket and when I come across difficult situations in my work (such as a recent job interview) I often ask myself, "What would Jim do?"

For me the most powerful thing Jim said was definitely, "Do something scary every day." Even if it's doing a regular journey in a different way, even if it's one step each day, it's a good principle and I still try to do it, even if it's something quite small. It's not just my professional life where things have changed, I've started doing things I'd been putting off in other areas of my life and my wife says (to her great delight) I've become far more impulsive (such as booking holidays at short notice) and now just 'go for it'. Once you've cured your fears, you feel like there's nothing you can't do.

My outlook now is to make a decision, stand by it, and tell others what you are going to do, then you are committed and have to see things through.

If last year's challenge was the presentation, this year it's learning Japanese. I collect retro video games and import many of them from Japan and therefore got interested in the language and culture through that, so now I'm learning to speak it. It will certainly help with reading the instruction manuals. We'll have to see what next year's challenge will be.

Chapter 11

Rule 8: Understand and control your time to create change

You and I have only one truly scarce resource. There is only one thing that we all run out of and we are utterly powerless to replenish. Whether you are a prince or a pauper, a CEO or a schoolchild, there is only one resource that you and I are depleting every moment of every day.

That scarce resource is time.

A Tiger tamer denies the possibility of 'spending' time doing this or that because 'spent' time cannot come back to affect us. 'Spent' time is gone. Our use of time always brings a return, there is always a consequence. So, we are 'investing' it in doing things, not 'spending' it. But in what things should we choose to invest? And is it you or the Tiger who dictates your investment decisions? Welcome to Rule 8:

Understand and control your time to create change.

If we gain control of time, we have a huge amount of it to invest, and we have a planet filled with extraordinary things and people to invest it in and with. And that includes our homes and that includes the workplace and, of course, everything else in between.

We are the sum of those investment decisions. The position that we find ourselves in today is the sum of how we have chosen to invest our time. And tomorrow we will add the consequence of the decisions that we are taking today. Now there's a thought. Even the children you have or may have in the future are the genetic result of whom you chose to invest time with on that second date as opposed to the ones you chose not to invest time with after date one!

Rule 8 for Taming Tigers is not about time management. It is about taking a fundamental shift in our relationship with time and then looking at the Tigers that stand between you and controlling your time. Rule 8 is a vital tool for change for individuals and groups (even organisations are just lots of individuals after all). It requires the would-be tamer of Tigers to look at time differently, to gain a new understanding of their personal relationship with time and choose whether that relationship is governed by the Tiger or by the individual's choice. Rule 8 is the second of the Change Rules and it will prove vital to really understand your relationship with time if you wish to create lasting change.

Economists use the idea of scarce resources and how we allocate or 'invest' them. So the first step here is to see if time really is yours to allocate, yours to invest. Then we can look at investment strategies. Economists also use the idea of 'opportunity cost', the missed opportunities that must be taken into account when an investment decision is taken. So the opportunity cost of my decision (and it is always my decision in the world of Taming Tigers — no victims permitted) to attend a meaningless meeting that requires a day's travel has an opportunity cost of not getting my new business case written, or not getting an appointment set to present it to the board, or not hitting my numbers and so on. We'll need these concepts of allocation of scarce resources and opportunity cost for this chapter.

After that, seeing as how this is a book about taking action, about doing stuff, it will then be necessary to begin to take new decisions, better decisions, about what you do with the time that you have.

Time and the victim

"But we don't control our time," he or she will contribute enthusiastically to a group discussion after a Taming Tigers presentation, desperate to get other heads to nod (and nod some, but only some, do), "If I had control over my time then I could . . . but I don't, so I can't! The speaker runs his own company, he doesn't understand what it's like for us!"

Oh how I wince — it's me! He is me at my desk in Slough watching the coffins go by. I know him so well it's like we're old pals. Or old adversaries, I'm never sure. I move to the next table in silence. Let's see if the group will turn itself around without me butting in.

This was my own favourite reason for not creating a change in the days before I got to recognize the Tiger. I was far too busy to squeeze it in and my time was certainly not my own, so what could I do? I was powerless, forced by "the system" to stay in an oh-so-cosy rut. The Tiger, having created the wonderful victim delusion, wanders back to his forest victorious and all can return to normal. None of it is my responsibility. I nearly used this as a Rulebook rule to get out of riding (see Rule 2). I had to pay the mortgage so how could I possibly find the time to ride horses every morning?

"Ah, relax. You don't have to," came my soothing reply to myself. "They'll understand". And, of course, they would have understood.

So, our victim of the system — a system he ironically condones by his very presence in the room — is using his considerable communication talents to convince a table of eight to twelve typically healthy and affluent members of one of the planet's richest nations that they are victims. They are working in an economic environment desperate for and willing to reward innovation and commitment. They have been brought together by the company to create new ideas and ways of progressing, and that company has invested in an entire afternoon of Tiger taming to demonstrate their commitment to their people to move forward, to give control to them, to ask for energy and excitement. But they are "powerless".

Despite all evidence to the contrary, "we don't have time and there's nothing we can do to change that" is the comment that we will hear at most tables in most companies. Many people are engaged in a passionate, desperate, wild and utterly vital love affair with the idea that they are too busy to do anything interesting or exciting and that time is not their own to invest.

Now, of course, the discussion doesn't end there, but that is surely where it begins. One of two things will now happen. Either the group will begin to moan collectively about their situation, or the tide will turn against our victim and somebody will point out that he is labouring under a Rule 2

'Rulebook' delusion. Somebody will gently suggest that the Tiger creates the victim's relationship with time and that it is done to keep him safe from risk or exposure.

And Taming Tigers has now assisted in creating that new relationship with time amongst groups as diverse as shop floor factory workers to top flight sales professionals to lawyers (often the very worst victims) to leaders in innovative media and IT businesses. And when you think about that — that the wealthy lawyers are generally far more inclined to be victims of this delusion than the factory worker who has to clock in and out and perform a function with (at first sight) very little room for personal creativity within it — the paw prints of the Tiger become obvious.

The excitement in the session comes not from seeing the shift in the relationship. That is a fleeting moment, a stepping stone across the river to the new pasture. The excitement comes with what people decide to do for their families and societies, colleagues and companies as a result. It's the fusion of Rule 8 and the individual's creativity that is the thrill. Realising that they are free — what will they do with their freedom?

The Tiger and our relationship with time

So how is the Tiger getting involved here? To answer that question, let's look at those Integrity Rules again. We'll start with Rule 2. The Rulebook — the source of so many problems.

The Rulebook, unless, of course, challenged hourly, is generally under the control of the Tiger. It keeps us safe, you will remember, and makes it all 'not our fault'. Well, by this stage in our trip, you can recognize that for yourself in the example above. It does not need great expansion here other than to point out that if you are investing your most scarce resource based on an invalid set of rules then you risk getting a tragically disappointing return on that investment.

If you upped the stakes, if you had to find the time to do the thing 'or else' [you can insert some dire consequence for yourself here], in this flight of imagination, how would the Rulebook immediately alter about time? How would your relationship with time and how you 'have' to invest it, shift?

Are we creating a Rulebook that enables us to act in integrity with ourselves, who we truly are and who we want to be (for our impact on others and our world as much as for ourselves)? Or a Rulebook that keeps us safe from the realities of acting with integrity?

And then we have to turn to Rule 3. If we have decided where it is we want to arrive at and we're working towards it, then Rule 8 is less relevant. But most people are not moving towards a place of their choosing and most people do not have a plan. Just watch them today.

Often a part of the Rule 3 planning process is the very act of making the time to do the things necessary to reach the goal. It is amazing how resourceful you can be at this once you have the goal in place. But this is all 'Long Term-High Risk' work, and we live in a 'Short Term-Low Risk' world, so most of us never allocate the time to do the planning (we'll explore these concepts together in a moment).

And of course, we then go back to Rule 1. Act boldly (to start doing the thing you want to be doing) because time is limited. Not only is the 'T' word, 'time' back in there explicitly, but all of Rule 1 is designed to shatter your Rulebook (Rule 2) and expose the Tiger at work. It is about wrestling your time back to yourself by using it to create a bold forward step — proving to yourself that you could have done it years ago and you can do it again tomorrow.

Investment strategies for time

Do you see time as something to be 'managed' or as the result of the amazing coincidence of you having life? A life that can be invested in creating all sorts of incredible things, from bringing energy and enthusiasm to teammates and colleagues to reshaping how your business or industry operates to nurturing your children or supporting a partner. And that's before you visit the Pyramids or run your marathon for charity!

We'll not get an overdraft on this resource that is time — no credit here — so it is well worth considering for a little while. That may be a worthwhile investment in itself. And what better time to consider it than now?

Here are four main ways that we can invest our time. I repeat, I'm using the word 'invest' here rather than 'spend' because each delivers a return for us. It is always there, invested behind us. Each of the four main investment routes delivers a different level of return. Every individual will invest in each area — it's part of being human. The game is balancing your investments rather than having the Tiger dictate the investment and the return. And what is the return? The return here is the quality of story that you are writing rather than permitting the Tiger to dictate to you, the sense of purpose that you are creating and satisfying, and the Tigers that you are Taming.

Short Term-High Risk investment decisions

These are the here and now concerns. They require attending to. These particular short term concerns are high risk to you because they matter. You can spot a short term decision because it has a deadline attached to it. The moment will pass.

It is high risk because, if you were to fail here, you would feel the consequences immediately and they would be significant. You may have to take a risk, also, to invest correctly in this area. Probably a personal risk involving a Tiger, whether the Tiger is faced in merely creating the time to do this thing right or the Tiger is in the action you have to take here. So the action itself may have a perceived high risk attached to it (the Rule 1 'bold action', for example).

The loved one who is taken ill requires a Short Term-High Risk investment of your time. Short term because it is now, and high risk to you, your loved one, and your perception of yourself if you fail to act. Probably high risk also as you will face the Tiger of letting others down at short notice to invest here. Similarly, with the member of the team who is in need of a confidence boost just before a meeting, it is now that you invest that time — now or never. It may matter to you for a whole host of commercial and personal reasons that you find the time to invest here, despite the inevitable opportunity cost of not investing that time where you had already planned to invest it.

We usually make the correct Short Term-High Risk investment decisions. They should not worry you too much except for the moments when you have a Short Term-Low Risk investment opportunity calling at you and you confuse which is the right path.

Short Term-Low Risk investment decisions

And here we have it. The great gloopy forgettable morass of dross-activity that takes the majority of our most precious and scarce resource, time.

These are short term concerns because they have a deadline attached and they are low risk to you because they do not matter. Nothing is at stake. So they are easy to perform and deliver little result. However much we stress and rush and forget to invest time for the long term, this is the stuff that we will have forgotten about by next week, let alone by the nursing home. Now I know that some of it has to be done, but the question is, how much? Which parts? And does the Tiger let you discriminate or tell you what's what?

In the second part of this chapter we will begin to create practical strategies for controlling your time. For now, it is important that you recognize it. It is the email inbox, it is the mobile phone, and it is the internal meeting without any true agenda and it is even, often, the external meeting.

If you want to look at the Short Term-Low Risk in high relief, try this:

Step one: Imagine that you have no salary (that'll not be too hard for the self-employed out there who are ahead of the game on this one. Ever seen a plumber in a meeting unless you were paying him to be there?). From now on you are only paid for the tangible benefits that you deliver for your organisation. The measurable results. And you are only paid for what they are worth to the organisation. This means that if you increase the quantity and quality of your results *you will get paid much more*. But if you invest your time driving around the country to attend a meeting without moving your results further to completion as a result, you will struggle to put food on the table quite soon. And did I mention the good bit? You do not have to go to any set location at any set time other than at your choice in order to achieve your result. Of course, part of 'your' result is also measured on the team's result, so cooperating with your colleagues and working as a part of the team is still in the deal, but only if the team is generating a result — not just to create occupied meeting rooms. You'll have to take real decisions about which team activities to support with your time.

Step two: Now write down in black what it is you did last week, the real activities that can be put into a diary. Only activities that directly account for your results, first. Next, add in what of your activities directly accounted for delivering team results.

Step three: Write in red all the stuff that you did last week that did not deliver or build towards a tangible result. Now, activities like coaching, communication and morale boosting only count towards the result if there was an agreed follow-up action and review procedure after the conversation. If not, *for the purpose of this exercise*, that's just chatting to people!

Step four: Cross out all the stuff in red that nobody in the world would miss. The 'agenda-free-Monday-Morning-Croissant-and-Coffee-fest-to-take-the-sting-out-of-Mondays Meeting' might be in there, for example. As might that trip for three hours each way in the car to attend a meeting that you could have attended for twenty minutes by phone if you'd only tamed the Tiger of ringing that senior person and asking why you were required there.

Step five: Cross out all of the stuff in red that, if you passed on to others, it would leave you free to achieve more through your particular talent for the team. This will, of course, involve confronting your 'delegation Tiger' or, if there is nobody to delegate to, meeting your 'hire someone so that I can get better results for the team' Tiger head on.

Step six: So, here's the exciting bit. How long would it take you to do what you did last week? And what would you, in a quiet moment of private honesty, pay yourself for the tangible result you produced? Half your salary? Twice your salary? If you are reading this and you are self-employed, given the real results that you delivered for customers or clients last week, are you amazed they paid you what they did or do you now want to value yourself at a higher rate?

What you have done is taken out all of your Short Term-Low Risk investments. You are left with your Short Term-High Risk Investments and you have room for some even higher risk Tiger Taming activities to go in there also. Now let's look at what this all means.

You may have found that you have a very healthy relationship with time and invest wisely in short term activities that produce results — the high risk activities. But many

people find that they can strip out a great deal of the things
that they do when they go through this exercise.

Of course, it's human nature to do many enjoyable,
relaxed activities with a low risk attached. It is why we email
rather than walk across the office to speak with somebody or
call them up. It is why we traipse off to the meeting rather
than call to ask why it is being held. I once attended a meeting of senior training professionals within a company where
we had three hours scheduled together. Only one of them
(the person who had arranged it) knew who I was or why I
was there. They had all travelled for hours across the UK to
attend. What motivated them to get into their cars?

There is a risk involved in avoiding the Short Term-Low
Risk investments of your precious resource. The Tiger is
lurking when you do. But there is also a route to a far higher
return on your investment. And remember, that return need
not be financial here. Taming this Tiger affords us time with
loved ones and the opportunity to use time rescued to pursue
new and more meaningful goals, both at work and at home.

Investing for the long term

It is very hard to focus those Short Term activities and take
wise and perhaps bold decisions regarding the allocation of
your precious, scarce resource without a long term strategy
to guide you. And yes, you've guessed it, that is worthy of
some time and thought under Rule 8.

Long Term-Low Risk investment decisions

Now let's define long term as anything that does not have a
forced deadline attached to it. Economists would certainly

argue with that one, but for the purpose of our exercise let's just keep it simple for a moment. And low risk, remember, means that the Tiger is not going to cause us any difficulty here. So unlike with a Short Term-Low Risk decision of how to invest our time, there is no deadline here. And there is no Tiger attached at any level to doing the thing. No danger of procrastination here, then. Nothing to fear in engaging with this activity.

Here, of course, we are into the realms of time invested staring at the television every evening. This is not about our leisure time, that's vital. No, this is the time that we would immediately cut into if we had a sense of purpose. It's the time spent with a bottle of wine, simply because we couldn't think of anything better to do than drink a bottle of wine. Not the time spent with a bottle of wine and a good friend — that's a totally different state of affairs.

You may think that daydreaming counts as a Long Term-Low Risk investment decision. You would be correct up to a point. Letting the mind wander to far off places in the sure knowledge that, if we have an idea that excites us whilst off on our dreaming, we will switch to a Long Term-High Risk strategy is no longer day dreaming. We're concerned in this section with the dreams that will never be acted upon. The dreams which the Tiger will put quietly back to sleep. The dreams that we would no more take a bold action to reach than we would drive our car into a cold lake. These dreams, of course, are entirely low risk. They're fantasies played out in the cinema of the mind.

But what could they be without the Tiger? Let's find out.

Long Term-High Risk investment decisions

So, again, we have no forced deadline attached to taking these decisions. Some people never take any. But once one of these decisions is taken and a deadline applied, now we have attached a risk! So the Tiger will snarl when we think about these things.

Committing to booking the holiday and taking vital rest time, either just for ourselves or in order to invest time with our friends or families, has certainly got some risk attached. You will need to take time out of the diary when you have no idea what your priorities will be out there in the future. You'll have to take some money out of the bank account and, worst of all, maybe find a half-day now in order to book it. But what an excellent investment of time it will be.

The time spent daydreaming about where you wish the future to take you — that's a worthwhile investment of time. As are daydreams about what the next challenge and goal is for you in your professional life, your family life or even your social and community life will be, deciding when you're going to write that book, or raise that money for charity, or start that course of study that you know is the next stage in your professional development.

But of course, we're in Tiger taming territory now. Now you are in danger of adventure and excitement. Now you know that the daydreams that you are dreaming are designed to be acted upon. Before you let the Tiger snarl at you and scale back your plans to a more pedestrian, mediocre, manageable level, daydream on! Maybe it's time to dream with a notepad in front of you and start putting down some of the small steps that might take you there.

Maybe it's time to daydream with Rule 2 for Taming Tigers in front of you, to write down all the reasons why you 'know' you cannot achieve your new daydream and then, one by one, to test them against the Rule 2 criteria. Can they be proven scientifically? Or are these assumptions you are making to keep yourself safe from risk? Safe from the Tiger?

It is time invested in this Long Term-High Risk investment vehicle that enables us to find the sense of purpose, define the goals and create the plan that we discussed under Rule 3. This in turn requires us to challenge the Rulebook that we met in Rule 2. This in turn demands that we create the bold action that we stumbled over when we first read Rule 1 and that we have now seen can produce some astounding results.

Perhaps it is in the Long Term-High Risk investment of time that we decide to take action against the voices in the head, pledge to look for the tools for Taming Tigers and to see if they really are, and always have been, all around us. Perhaps it is in this area that we begin to finally become excited about the fact that there is no safety in numbers, and that we are now preparing to leave the pack and strike out on our own. We are finally going to do something scary, and it feels good. Here we can begin to plot the disciplines that we shall put in place and decide whether or not we are committed to this thing, whether or not we are going to keep doing things until the thing is done.

And the next day, when the planning is done, we will need to start working in Short Term-High Risk mode when we allocate time. And that will involve facing the Tiger and having some unusual conversations.

But don't worry, there are some more tools available to help you start your new adventure.

Controlling your time to create change

As Rule 8 suggests, it comes in two halves. The first half is a careful look, perhaps for the first time, at your relationship with time in order to 'understand' time. The second, of course, is practical guidance on how then to start to 'control' your time to create change.

People are often surprised that I claim to have learned so much about the Ten Rules for Taming Tigers from watching jockeys. I daresay I could have learned a great deal from watching top flight entrepreneurs or world class engineers, but it happened to be jockeys. Now what do you think would possess a young jockey who is not particularly wealthy, but who is desperate to succeed in his career to engage a fulltime driver and reduce his take-home pay to the breadline? Kudos? I don't think so. Jockeys are masters and mistresses of investing their time. Let me explain why.

As you know by now, a jockey's day starts at around 5am. He's not eating much and it may be the middle of winter, but off he goes to ride out a couple of jumpy horses in the rain or the fog, often for free, in order to keep relations good with a particular trainer. He then drives to the races, which may well be a three or four hour drive. Whilst in the car, he will be making calls to trainers — he is his own most effective salesperson, after all — and taking calls from his agent, who books rides on his behalf. He will be calling other jockeys who have ridden horses that he will ride today to understand how best to handle them, and he might even find time to call his friends and family. Then he gets to sit in a sauna for a couple of hours to dehydrate his body to the required weight.

Then it's six races back-to-back, maybe hitting the deck at around thirty miles per hour from six or more feet off the ground, with just enough time to change silks and perhaps have the odd cup of sugary tea during the course of the afternoon to keep him going. And when he's at the races, between rides, he will also want to make time to catch up with any owners or trainers who are at the racecourse whom he needs to maintain good relations with. Then it's the three or four hour journey back, possibly without any more than a banana to eat.

When he gets home, he may have to burn off some calories or he may have to sweat in the bath and, of course, some time with his family would be nice. Then it is time to polish his riding-out boots for the morning and take himself off to bed. And the next day he does it all again. And the day after that he does it all yet again. And the next day he . . .

So, now we can begin to see why the jockey will invest in a driver. It's because there is only so much time for him to invest in twenty-four hours and he wants to invest it in being the very best he can possibly be in his profession. And that profession requires a lot of driving to be done, which is the only job that can be delegated. And so he either does that driving, with the mental strain it leaves on him as he arrives at the races and the time that it takes up, or he climbs into the back of the car, makes his calls and gets some sleep.

But, think about it. It's a bold decision to hire a driver. Jockeys aren't rich people — you'll hear about the top four or five, but you won't go much further than that before you'll find someone who'll struggle from time to time. They may well be earning less than you, but it is important enough to them that their travelling doesn't impede their work that they will tame the finance Tiger in order to invest their time as they believe they need to. Would you?

What are the Tigers that stop you taking the decisions that enable you to invest your time the way that you need to? It really is worth considering. But now that we've tried to 'understand time' (without the help of Einstein, admittedly), it is time to look at some of the ways you can battle to gain control of the 'time Tiger'.

Tools to gain control of your time

Tool one: The diary

Now here's a thought:

Your position now = the sum of your choices to date;

Your choices = your actions and inactions;

Your actions and inactions = where time is invested
and effort applied — or not;

Where time is invested and effort applied or not = your diary;

Therefore,

Your diary today = your position tomorrow?

Now, this may not be mathematically convincing, but it is a thought, and I find it a powerful one.

Have another read and see if the importance of your diary and what you choose to keep out of it — and, perhaps more fascinatingly, who is choosing what goes into or stays out of it — is an accurate description of where you were *choosing* to apply your time and energy. Is it, therefore, a plan of your upcoming actions?

And do you agree that your actions are what have put you in the position you are in now? And please open this wide up, we don't need to just look at your work diary when considering the answer to this. If you diarised all the activities that you do out of work, would you see High Risk-Long and Short term investments in there?

So here's how to use this tool. Diarise everything for a short while. Pay close attention to how things arrive in there. Pay close attention to whether there is any time being allocated for the Long Term-High Risk activities that we agreed were so vital in writing your story. Once that has been done, you can decide whether the exercise was a total waste of time, has made you think and realise a few things so you can now stop doing the exercise, or whether, in fact, you want to keep using your diary as your tool and as your conscience, and monitor carefully your portfolio of time investments.

Tool two: Tame the "no" Tiger

Saying "no" can be extremely difficult. Saying no to senior people or aggressive people in the workplace can be exceptionally difficult. Negotiating with the family can sometimes be a minefield through which we don't particularly want to tread. However, saying "no" is probably the single most important Tiger to tame in terms of time control. And the Ten Rules for Taming Tigers will help you to say "no" to people.

What I mean is this: If you have a clear sense of purpose and have become emboldened by that sense of purpose, if you have a plan in place to get there and are looking all around you for the tools, if you have re-written elements of your Rulebook and have dealt with the voices, then people start to see you differently. You have become the person that we examined in Chapter 6 when we looked at Rule 3 (Head in the direction of where you arrive, every day). *You have become the inspirational person with the light shining in their eyes.*

Now you are a different force to be reckoned with. Trust me. You are in a different place and you can now say "no". Also, and very importantly, you will know *why* you are saying "no" and you will be able to articulate to them precisely why you are saying "no". And if that 'why' has been arrived at in integrity and is being followed in integrity, they will only push back at you if there is an extremely good reason why they need your assistance. And in that case, it is probably a very good idea to stop and listen.

And, for those who have spent their lives enjoying and hanging on desperately to their difficulty in saying "no" and the self esteem issues which drive them to please everybody around them, here is a suggestion: Harsh as it may sound, you are not pleasing others, you are pleasing yourself. You are doing exactly what you are choosing to do — living a life blaming others' unreasonableness (and your saintly disposition, of course) for the position that your investment of time has brought you to. A life without the courage to cause 'minor conflict' when it is perfectly reasonable and, perhaps on occasion, morally right to do so.

It will never be easier to stand up and be counted and tomorrow feels just like today. So try a "no" the next time you feel it is right. Try it politely, try it with a smile and with a rational reason as to why it has been said. It could be a very, very exciting moment when the other person simply nods, agrees and finds somebody else to help them.

Tool three: Tame the 'time bandit' Tiger

The 'time bandits' have long been a staple on every time management course, so I won't dwell on them here. You know who I mean: they do not have a sense of purpose, and sometimes they seem to have little sense of right or wrong as they casually accept a pay cheque (and their full "entitlement" to sick pay) for their hard work in disrupting the people around them. You'll rarely find a self-employed time bandit, by the way.

If you've got this far in the book and you're creating a new sense of purpose for yourself, you won't need any help from me in Taming the Tiger of dealing with the time bandit. All I would like to do is offer you a few words of encouragement: Yes, you are doing the right thing. Get away from them. Avoid them at lunchtime and, if necessary, move your desk to another part of the country to get out of the way of their vacuous noise. And yes, I too have been caught in the error of thinking that it was my human duty to listen to them, as if I were performing the role of some kind of unpaid therapist. But the thing is, the patient never gets better. The more you listen, the worse the disease gets!

Give yourself permission to get them out of your way. Excellent. Let's move on . . .

Tool four: Tame the gadget Tiger

Nothing distracts me like the gentle alarm of an email arriving. How about you? Can you resist taking a look? Now let's just assume that it is actually a work-related email, isn't it tempting to respond? And what happened to that sense of purpose? What happened to that deep thread of thought, that carefully allocated and diarised investment of Short Term-High Risk time that you were engaged in?

Turn your emails off. Turn your mobile off. Throw your PDA in the river, is there really any excuse for them? Turn them back on at the appointed time in your diary for dealing with communication. It's the only chance you will have in the modern world of ringtones and wireless broadband (liberating though this is) to engage your brain for any period of time and drive your world forward on your terms. Surely the badge of honour is not availability and speed of response. The badge of honour is great results. The former only matters as a genuine facilitator of the latter — other than common courtesy, of course. And common courtesy also dictates that we should not expect a response from people holidaying with their children for a fortnight.

And by the way, if you're ever in a meeting that's so unimportant that people are tapping on laptops and checking PDAs rather than attending to the subject matter, the meeting is a waste of time and of the associated travel time. Tame that Tiger straightaway. Leave!

Tool five: Use Deadlines

The key to the short term investment is the enforced deadline. The definition of the long term activity is that it has no deadline until we create one ourselves. There is nobody requiring that you plan your next career move or plan your holiday. Until that deadline has been set — by you — it remains a daydream or a doodle on a notepad. Until that is done, you can blame the fact that your dream has not come true on your bad luck, but that is unlikely to help you much.

And make the deadline public, put something at stake against it, make it necessary that you hit the deadline or that email will pop up and distract you just as you are beginning to make progress. The greatest risk in investing time is that irrelevant activities with noisy deadlines sap the time that should have been allocated to the important activities — like telling fairy tales to your children or planning how to grow your business or department — that had no deadline put against them publicly, but had a very real deadline against them in terms of the story of our lives. Tick. Tock.

Tool six: Put aside planning time

This has been addressed above, but it's vital to list it as a tool for controlling your time. Once you remember to put dreaming and planning times along with associated deadlines into your diary (you can disguise it as walking the dog or taking a bath if you wish), you begin to create and become excited by change in your life. And as soon as you start acting on that path, it's different for you. You're meeting different people. It really wasn't that difficult. It never was. It was simply that this little bit of dreaming and planning time has only just, perhaps for the first time, perhaps not, been given pride of place in your diary.

Tool seven: Try the nursing home test, monthly

Many, many pages ago, we started out our discussion together by acknowledging the fact that we would like to be happy, nimble old people, living in the nursing home. Many years away, for sure, but nonetheless better that, I presume, than any alternative. So maybe now, as we consider how to invest the time that will pass between this point in our lives and the time when we will get to master our domino skills, we should give the nursing home our thoughts once again.

What does the man or the woman looking into that mirror wish that the man or woman that is reading this book at this moment in time was doing differently? What can they see as the possibilities, the immense opportunities that, perhaps, were squandered in the 'folly of youth'? Oh, and by the way, the 'folly of youth' of this happy, nimble old ninety year old person reaches up until your 80th birthday!

Maybe you should take that happy old person's advice on investing our most scarce commodity.

Finding the time to become a jockey

I had to pay the mortgage. So whilst others went racing to win money after riding out. I went off to work to find it.

I have referred to the importance of time to the racing project elsewhere (see Chapter 6, Rule 3) and don't propose to repeat myself here. It will be enough to say that without this Rule and Michael Caulfield's blunt and accurate advice, I would have failed long, long before I mastered the rising trot. The lessons I learned about the value of my time and how to control it caused me to get creative and restructure my entire business to release some of my most scarce resource, time. To make the Short Term-High Risk investments that I required for the Long Term-High Risk investment strategy of race riding. The resultant use of partners and using efficient, diverse routes to market dictate how I structure my business to this day.

There is only one truly scarce resource.

You are investing it now.

Be sure that you are deciding the investment strategy your-self and that you like the look of the return.

Got that diary handy?

Case study: Steve Holliday

I work with a number of books and coaching models and only recently heard Jim speak and there are several of his Rules that I can relate to in terms of the journey I've been going on over the past few years.

> *"Time is one of your most valuable assets. I've realised that you can't do everything in a senior job, what you can do is a small number of big things. Do 3 or 4 key things that will have a knock on effect and you'll make better use of time."*

I was in the pharmaceuticals and medical devices business until about eighteen months ago. About three or four years ago, I was selected to go on a business coaching programme and for the first time I started to career manage. I learned ways of thinking and behaving to produce different results. I realised I was capable of more and started to manage my career. Most importantly, I learned the difference between management and leadership. I started reading books by people such as Steven Covey and more recently, I have been working with a personal coach who is a psychologist.

I now work as Head of Health and Safety for the power station division at E.ON. I started out in Operations, but I have been a Health and Safety professional now for twelve years. I only became chartered three years ago but because of Jim and others I have been speaking to recently, I decided to change back to Operations. The power of Jim's advice is once your direction is clear, this can be a powerful magnet, so I'm setting myself in a new direction.

In my personal life, I've had an experience similar to Jim's jockeying; it happened after an old friend had skin cancer. He recovered, but our group of friends decided to do something for the hospital that had looked after him. We decided to do a coast to coast bike race in three days to raise money. Initially I made excuses. I thought it wouldn't be possible and I wouldn't have time as I hadn't been on a bike in years. What motivated me was that we trained as a group of friends; it was about doing something together. The first year we did the ride in three days.

Two years later, we managed it in two days. It comes back to Jim's principle, if you even think that you would like to do it, you can do it. But the Tigers are quick to come and say, "You can't do that." That point struck home for me and I've been thinking about it. Last night I was with my friends and we got talking; now we're thinking about doing John O'Groat's to Land's End next year, and I haven't been on a bike since the last trip, but having achieved what we have already, it is possible.

The Rules I identify with most are numbers 1, 3, 4, 5, 7, 8 and 10. Of these, Rules 1, 3 and 7 are most important to me. For me, 'act boldly today' is about recognising time as one of your most valuable assets. I've realised that you can't do everything in a senior job, what you can do is a small number of big things. Do three or four key things that will have a knock-on effect and you'll make better use of time. I have the work-life challenge too as I want to be a good husband and father and friend.

Jim talks about how there are voices in your head. As you start coaching, you become more aware of these voices saying, "I'm not sure I can do that, maybe it's too big a stretch". If you don't get your mind round that first Tiger — is it possible or not? — and do things that are uncomfortable, you will never find out. I'm different now because I have a better understanding of my personal development. It isn't always easy, I think you need to plan for feeling challenged and be prepared for it.

Rule 3 is about moving towards the goal you want to achieve. I was doing some coaching with a friend this morning, who is having problems at work. He knew what to do and what outcome he wanted but couldn't say so to his line manager. I gave him Jim's card with the Ten Rules. I suggested that he identify the top three companies he wanted to work for and talk to them. He thought I was joking, but I meant it. You need to be clear on what defines success in life, work and personal relationships and move towards it. It's like Jim and the jockeying. He clearly got over the Tiger and went every day in that direction. For me making sure people are clear on their goals and the direction they are moving is the biggest challenge for any organisation.

Rule 7 is about doing something bold every day, but it doesn't always have to be big things. Sometimes doing something quite small can be bold, and change can be incremental, as long as it's moving in the right direction every day.

Jim's Rule 5 is about finding the tools that will help. For me it was the coaching. One thing I've learned is that it's important to learn the individual characteristics and ways of working with your colleagues. Everyone has different models they find helpful.

Rule 10, 'Never, never give up', is something I agree with, but it is difficult at times.

Having learned so much through coaching myself, I've become interested in enlightening others. Going through extensive coaching makes you think you could be good at it yourself and so you want to try it, and to help with coaching programmes and leadership days.

Chapter 12

Rule 9: Create disciplines — do the basics brilliantly

When I first started out on my bet to prove that the Rules for Taming Tigers really worked, there were only eight rules. I learned Rules 9 and 10 during the course of that year.

Now, I know that discipline is a really unsexy word to most people in the twenty-first century. But I think we're missing a big trick if we don't take a little look at that old fashioned idea. Let me try and persuade you of that with a story.

There is a famous jockey called Frankie Dettori, probably the most famous jockey on planet Earth today, most certainly one of the most successful in the history of horse-racing. But as at the beginning of June 2007 (Frankie's twenty-third year as a professional jockey) he had not won perhaps the most coveted race in Europe, the English Derby at Epsom. On 2nd June 2007, Frankie Dettori took a little colt named Authorized to post in the Derby. He cantered to the post with something approaching eighty million pounds of bets placed on him and his little horse by the general public in the United Kingdom. Now even though it may not take Frankie long, on his diet, to fill his supermarket trolley on a Saturday evening, you wouldn't really want to appear in the local supermarket at all if you had disappointed a betting public that large. So with that much pressure on his shoulders, but with his usual professional coolness, Frankie and Authorized were loaded into the starting stalls for the one mile, four furlong and ten metre classic of classics.

As the field jumped out, Frankie kept his mount towards the rear and switched the talented little horse off, allowing him to bowl along, letting the lead horses do all the hard work over the undulating Epsom track. But by the time they reached the famous Tattenham Corner and begun to turn for home, Frankie had asked Authorized to show to the watching millions just how talented he was. And, slowly at first, the horse gathered up the galloping field until, by the time he reached the beginning of the grandstands, Authorized and Frankie were in an unassailable position for the Italian to claim his first English Derby. And so, the man who had broken records by winning all seven races on a single race card at Ascot in 1996 added the single remaining prize he most wanted to complete an enviable collection of the world's most valuable classic horserace trophies on his mantelpiece. Lucky Frankie Dettori.

The whip was waved at the crowd, the smile beamed and the famous flying dismount was delivered to cheers in the Winner's Enclosure. But that wasn't enough for Mr Dettori, so that evening he flew to France to pair up the next day with another talented colt, Lawman to win the Prix du Jockey

Club (the French equivalent of the English Derby). Lucky Frankie Dettori.

Now I don't know what you call that, but I call winning two Derby's in one weekend just plain greedy! So Mr Dettori flew home to his lovely house and his lovely wife, all the little Dettorinis running around at knee-height, two sparkling new Derby trophies for the mantelpiece and the prospect of some healthy prize money coming his way when the banks opened in the morning. Lucky Frankie Dettori!

But is Frankie Dettori lucky?

Let's have a look at a sample diet and a sample daily schedule for racing on the flat. I got my weight down to eight stone ten pounds from twelve stone using this diet but that is far too heavy for a real flat jockey. Taller men than me riding on the flat (I am five foot seven inches tall) would weigh much less than that.

You are up at 5am and at work for 6am. Racing doesn't do 'late' and it doesn't do 'sick'. But it does do a seven day week seeing as there are animals to be cared for and seeing as the betting public like to have seven days of racing.

Now, on a fine morning, nothing beats it, but in England, mornings are not always fine. So you can well be leaving the house in horizontal rain or chipping the ice from the windscreen at 5.30am. Before you go you'll want something in you to keep you going and a banana and a coffee (black no sugar) is par for the course. After three or four hours of riding out you're ready for some more to eat so another banana slips down a treat!

Why all the bananas? Well, I guess I'd better tell you what is off the menu and it might begin to make sense. I was given help on this by a sports scientist named Jon Pitts and here is what we cut out from my diet: All dairy produce, white pasta, bread, almost all red meat, all oils and most sauces, alcohol, muesli and nuts, all sweets and chocolate and biscuits and cakes. Chips were missed and curries were *really* missed. Dried fruit (unsweetened) is an occasional and very indulgent treat — replacing Minstrels as my companion on a long car journey. Obviously things like mayonnaise are out also — that didn't bother me but just try finding a sandwich on the road without that stuff in it!

So you are looking forward to lunch and, having ridden for much of the morning, lunch is nearly here. A small baked potato and lots of fresh salad. Obviously without the butter, beans, cheese, salad dressing and so on that might have been there in the old days. It is now that you begin to wonder how you never before discovered the delights of a squeeze of lemon! Why did you not pay more attention to the pepper pot and its little flakes of flavour? And where has mustard been all these years?

And you do keep to the diet. It's the job. And just so you know, the Clerk of the Scales does not say "look out son, those silk breeches are getting a bit tight, time to lay off the pies for a bit!" No, he sits you on the scales and if you weigh too much he calls up his good friend Mr Commentator who announces to the crowd that a particular jockey is overweight as he rides past them all with his backside in the air!

Your afternoon snack is an apple and then it's time to look forward to your dinner. Now your dinner needs to be eaten by 7.30pm as you need to have as little as possible in your system by bedtime. A chicken breast, skinned and grilled accompanied by some steamed vegetables is a welcome sight. And once it has settled, on go the running shoes to work off the day's intake and keep your fitness up. I had a long way to go with my fitness, so most evenings were spent with running shoes on. Others prefer to walk (for fear of putting muscle on their legs by running) or to work on the rowing machine.

Then you get up and do it again.

For the sake of completeness here, I should add that jockeys do very little resistance (weights) work. But clearly they need strength. You do not build strength in a finish from riding on the gallops as you don't push a horse out like that at home. Those who ride every day at the races tend to build and keep their strength just by doing the job. People returning from injury or who ride rarely at the races (or have never ridden there, like me) use something called an equicizer. It's like a grownup's rocking horse that mimics the resistance points that a jockey will have to push against in their arms and legs.

Gee introduced me to Jason Cook, a rider and fitness expert at the Lambourn Gym. Jason worked on my fitness with me a great deal and I owe him and Gee a debt for the fact that I looked in any way convincing on my first race. Jason had me on the gym's equicizer three times a week for months before the big day. The burn that you feel in your quad muscles on the equicizer has to be felt to be believed, but it's even more intense at the races so it has to be done. How I grew to dread the sessions with Jason, his stopwatch and the equicizer. How I was glad of the three of them at Southwell! We had put the disciplines in place and they paid me back.

A great deal of work is also done on balance and core strength at the gym, so hours were spent wobbling about on swiss balls until, many months later, I could kneel on one whilst juggling. I never have attempted to kneel on a horse and juggle but I was grateful for the balance and strength it gave me when, from time to time and with no warning, something spooked a horse whilst I was on board and he tried to disappear in a flash from underneath me.

Of course, for the real jockeys, every afternoon, after riding out and whilst sticking to the diet, is spent racing. During my year getting to the track, the day outside of riding out, diet and exercise was spent working for my business.

Lucky Frankie Dettori?

I played at that diet and that schedule for one year. Frankie and the others don't play at it. They work at it. And Frankie has worked at it for well over twenty-three years with consistent effort and discipline. And then there are the contacts nurtured, the skills in the saddle honed, the ability to get back on the horse every time it fires him off. And then there are the race tactics and the ability to read the race unfolding around you at great speed and to have studied and understood the form of the horses in the race and calculate what any jockeys decision might mean to you and your horse given the horse that he is on.

Luck? Probably not.

No, I don't think it's fair to say, "lucky Frankie Dettori." It is easy, when all we see is the flamboyant Italian take the roar of the crowd, the flying dismount, the trophy presentation and the headlines, to confuse over two decades of disciplined hard work with luck.

Is it easier for those we see at the top of their games, in any field — business, sport, parenting or academia — to stick to the daily disciplines that underpin their success than it is for us mere mortals? Probably not. They have taken a choice, decided what the disciplines will be to support that choice, and set about incorporating them into their daily lives.

But when we look at those top performers, in whatever field, and wonder if we too could work on those disciplines, the Tiger will attack and give us good reasons not to try. Let's explore some together for a moment.

"It's easy for them — if I were playing for those high stakes, I could be disciplined too!"

But the rewards were not always high for them! Once upon a time, every famous sportsperson was a highly disciplined 'unheard of', trying to get opportunities. They had these disciplines in place way before even that phase in their lives, a phase when they are getting very little reward or recognition for working daily at this discipline, when it is very hard to sustain (especially for the teenage jockey when their friends are off to the pub and they have both calories and a 5am start to think of).

"Obviously, discipline is important for a top sportsperson, but it makes no difference to me!"

Well spot that Tiger keeping you safe from grafting! Sure, whilst the results of discipline are obvious and high profile in some cases, and less obvious and less high profile in the case of you and me, the consequences are nonetheless there for us also. Look around. The people who put disciplines in place around their finances five, ten, fifteen, thirty years ago reap the reward of that discipline, don't they? The people who put discipline around the time they spend working to be great parents reap the rewards, don't they? You can add to that list yourself. Tigers to be tamed.

And what about work? As we look at the achievers that we admire, what are their little rules about the basics of excellent performance in the job?

"Whoa! This is not about Taming my Tiger! This is about achieving goals and results!"

Well, as I said previously, all of this can be used to achieve goals so, yes, it's a handy tool. But that is not why this is included as Rule 9 — it certainly is a way of taming your Tiger. Let me explain.

The Tiger is the thing that stops you, says "I couldn't" or "I shouldn't". So it is very useful, as you embark on the battle with your Tiger, to notice that it is those who *did* make a commitment to putting certain disciplines in place and to practising those brilliantly every day who have reaped the rewards. That they are mortal too, but they chose to put certain rules in place for themselves. Now that might, just might, inspire optimism in the battle against the Tiger when otherwise he would have defeated us.

Is there not a discipline around creating a balance between work and non-work that you can reap rewards from introducing? Is there not a discipline around putting nutritious food into our bodies that we will reap rewards from for years to come? This is not just about the CV achievement — although it can be.

So, let's get to the core of this with a deceptively simple question for you: Thinking about the story that you want to write, the life that you want to be living by now and the opportunities that you have no intention of missing in the future as you may have missed in the past, what disciplines do you think, had you put them in place ten years ago, would have altered the position that you are in today had you practised them faithfully on a daily basis?

If you put those disciplines in place for the next ten years, starting from today, how much of a difference do you think you would create in your life as a result of the sentence that you are writing in your head at this precise second? If you're not writing a sentence at this moment, put the book down and go for a walk. Do it now, have a little think. A decent plot in a film or in a book turns on a sentence, and this is a moment for sentence-writing.

If your head is popping, then take this one simple thought out on a walk with you instead: What is the one thing, the single thing that, if you did it brilliantly, every day of your life, would give you the biggest single difference in one week, one month, one year and beyond? What is the discipline you need to put in place and live and die by in order to write the story that you want to be writing?

How do you tack up a racehorse?

When my bet was made, back when there were only Eight Rules for Taming Tigers, I was not a big fan of discipline. "If it works for today, use it" was more my attitude. Gee didn't share that view! You ride out every day. You watch your weight every day. You run every day. There is no tomorrow to catch these things up. You can't 'cram' in this game!

I can still remember the look on Gee's face on the rare occasions when I would confess to her that, through pressure of work, I had only run twice that week or only ridden out four times. There would not be many of them, but when they came, the look of bemusement followed by disappointment, was dreadful.

And there are certain basics that we all need to define and then make it our business to excel at as part of this overall discussion of discipline. The little things that we make it our business to get right as part of the job. The foundations. The basics. It didn't take me long to cotton on to the seemingly tiny fact that every professional jockey who arrived at a yard I was riding out at, arrived looking neat as a new pin. Good quality, clean breeches, no horse slobber on their jacket and a shiny, if very worn, pair of boots. That was one to copy, then.

Another basic which I guess should have been obvious after my trip to Jamie Osborne's was that jockeys know how to tack up a horse. I didn't. Gee and I were talking about this and she decided that we couldn't wait for weeks to go by as I learned this on the job, day by day, holding people up as I went. So a call was made to Martin Bosley, "May we borrow Franklin Lakes next Saturday after he's exercised?"

"What for?" was the reasonable response.

"Tacking up practice!"

And so that was the following Saturday's project. Three hours of tacking and untacking — against Gee's stopwatch — on a nippy January day. I was later able to give more than one trainer the impression that I was better than I was by turning up looking lean and fit, dressed like a new pin and being first tacked up. "He must be good" was the illusion. And, as long as they didn't put me on the trickiest ride in the yard, I generally got away with it.

What are the rules that you need to put in place for yourself if you really want to get there?

In the story that you want to write, in the courageous campaign to eradicate all "what if's" and "if onlys" from the nursing home, sit for a moment. Really, just for a moment, and try again to answer this question to your own satisfaction:

What is the one thing, the single thing that, if you did it brilliantly every day of your life, would give you the biggest single difference in one week, one month, one year and beyond? What is the discipline you need to put in place and live and die by in order to write the story that you want to be writing?

If you can make time for thirty minutes TV a day, you could make time to be a very handy pianist in a couple of years, or to be a person who takes thirty minutes exercise every day and weighs many pounds less. It is the every day thing that matters. And it is the sticking with it.

You never know, in 23 years you could be winning win two Derbies in a weekend.

Case study: Lotta Vilde Wahl

My story is slightly different as I didn't discover the Ten Rules for Taming Tigers through hearing Jim speak. I met Jim in August 2007 when we were both attending a freediving course in Dahab in Egypt. Freediving is a sport where participants try to dive to deep depths without breathing apparatus. It was a beginner's course and I was trying it out for the first time.

"To train for the championships, I needed to develop a very disciplined approach. I was only able to take flexible jobs so that I could take time to go to Dahab, where I prefer to train. I also had to change my diet."

Jim told me the story about how he had become a jockey in a year in response to an audience member's challenge at one of his talks. He told me about the Ten Rules for Taming Tigers and how he had applied them in order to achieve his goal of becoming a jockey. I was very interested and ended up discussing it with some friends at dinner that evening. We all got very excited and decided to set ourselves personal challenges to achieve over the next two years. We decided to meet again at the end of the two years and share how we had got on with them.

Although I had only just started freediving, I really enjoyed it so the challenge I set myself was to take up the sport competitively and take part in the World Championships. I was thirty-eight years old and a lecturer and writer in Human Rights so although I kept in shape, I was not exactly an athlete! So there were a few Tigers to tame as I committed to working for a place on my National team.

When I got back home to Sweden, I joined the Swedish Freediving Association and enrolled in a course to improve my skills. When I told them about my ambition to dive at international level within two years, they laughed at me. The instructor of the course was very harsh. He mocked me at every opportunity and constantly told me I was useless. It was hard to cope with and it made me angry. I thought I must be doing very poorly, and I sometimes felt like giving up, but I was determined to tame the Tiger and succeed.

At the end of the course, we went for a meal, and my harsh instructor asked me to join the National team for the World Championships. I thought he was joking, I just couldn't believe it, but he was serious. At this time, I was able to dive to twenty-four metres. He set me a challenge of being able to reach thirty metres by the time of the championships in order to make the team. In the end, I exceeded his expectations and achieved forty metres!

I hadn't realised at the time, but I obviously had a talent for diving because it was very unusual to be able to dive to that depth after taking up the sport only three months before. Because my instructor was so tough, I thought I wasn't that good, but when I found myself on the team for the championships I knew I must be. After that, my coach was much more humble and told me it had taken him years to get to the stage I had got to in a month.

In order to train for the championships, I needed to develop a very disciplined approach. I was only able to take flexible jobs so that I could take time to go to Dahab, where I prefer to train. I also had to change my diet, as if you eat too soon before training it can make you ill. I had to cut out dairy products as they have an adverse affect when you are training, as well as all toxins such as alcohol.

At the World Championships, I was very nervous and I felt overwhelmed by everyone watching me and my first dive didn't go well. Fortunately, the second went much better and I was placed fourteenth out of twenty-four and I had achieved what I had set out to do in two years in a matter of months. That might make it seem like it was easy, but there were lots of challenges on the way and the Ten Rules for Taming Tigers helped me. In particular, Rule 3 (Head in the direction of where you want to arrive, every day), and Rule 7 (Do something scary every day) have been the most useful to me and have become my mantras.

When I was a child, a friend's father used to tell me, "act from courage, not fear" and I think that's what the Ten Rules for Taming Tigers help me to do.

I plan to return to the World Championships next year and achieve a better placing, perhaps even a medal.

Part Five

The Esteem Rule

Chapter 13

Rule 10: Never, never give up

Rule 10 of the Ten Rules for Taming Tigers stands alone. It was the last rule to be invented, and I'll tell you how it came to be added to the list in just a moment. I'd always been aware that staying power might be important, but I had thought that this sat within Rule 4 (It's all in the mind), dealing with setbacks and choosing your attitude. I was wrong. There's something deeper and more fundamental about the dogged determination that's necessary. And I discovered that during my year preparing to race and by meeting some of the extraordinary people I was lucky enough to meet during that time and since.

Rule 10 stands alone also as the Esteem Rule.

It's the finishers' Rule. It's the rule that separates the men from the boys, the women from the girls. It's the rule that is understood by people who've had to stand alone when all around them doubted them. They've stood firm, not arrogant, but firm. I don't think that I'd really found myself in a position where I had had to do that until the racing year.

It's the Esteem Rule because a degree of our esteem comes from what we have achieved. I mean this in a wider sense than what has been placed on your CV. If we've decided to always do the right thing by our families and we've never given up on that, we derive as much esteem as we would by deciding to pass an exam or run a marathon and not giving up on that. The point is that we said it, we worked at it and we did it — whatever 'it' might be and whatever the Tiger threw at us along the way.

It is the Esteem Rule because it wins us the esteem of others also. The world is full of grandstand jockeys. The world is full of people who could change the world if they only had a little more time. The world is not full of the people who commit to doing something and then see it through to its conclusion to the best of their abilities, taming unknown and unseen Tigers along the way. And other people know that. And that is why we gain the respect of others through Rule 10. After all, which of your heroes, the people who have really influenced you, have a reputation for leaving the job half done?

And finally, before we go racing together, there is a big difference between giving up and changing course. We might change course many times, perhaps radically, in order to reach the stated goal. There is no disgrace at all in coming down the mountain a few hundred feet in order to find a safer, smoother route to the summit.

One evening, about six months into the bet, Gee's brother, Marcus (who had won the Grand National in 1990 on Mr Frisk) had an idea, "Aren't you ready to ride in a charity race, yet?"

Unfortunately, Gee was within earshot and was onto the idea like a terrier. The evening was taking an alarming turn. Within thirty minutes, my fate was sealed. I was riding in a charity race in four weeks time at Brighton race course.

On the day of the race, I woke up at around 4am and was unable to get back to sleep. I was terrified. Unlike most racecourses, Brighton racecourse does not run a complete circuit; it is shaped like a warped horseshoe. This is not good for the novice whose horse may well bolt on the way to post. The runaway horse does not run wildly around a circuit until it exhausts itself. No. The horse runs to the end of the track where it meets "the cheesegrater".

The jockeys in the pub had had a glint in their eyes as they told me about 'the cheesegrater'.

"It's like the big white wooden screen thing they put behind the batsman on a cricket pitch," they said. "If a horse has lost the plot, they just run straight into it. Basically, if you get run off with on the way to post, you smash through the cheesegrater and you land up falling into the grounds of Roedean School for Girls. But if you can't pull up fast enough at the end of the race, you go through the other cheesegrater and land up on the beach!"

Gee and I drive to the racecourse. She's taken the day off to support me. I feel honoured but then have a sudden thought that she may well have come to make sure that I actually get onto the horse.

In the preceding weeks, Gee took me to Newbury race-track and we went through everything that I needed to know about procedure at the races. To the delight of the bored security guards watching over the otherwise empty race-course, she's had me come out and place my whip and hat silk onto the table in front of an imaginary Clerk of the

Scales. She's had me sit on the scales (until about a year ago, most scales at British Racecourses had a chair on them which the jockey sits upon holding all his tack) and solemnly announced my weight to me. And she's made me hand my tack to her (as she ran round to become the trainer rather than the Clerk of the Scales) and then go back into the weighing room for an imaginary cup of tea until she came in to call me for the race. Then we marched out to the empty parade ring together.

So, I am prepared for all eventualities. Except for Frankie Dettori and Jamie Spencer coming out of the weighing room in their silks for their last race as I walk in to change. Frankie gives me a nod as we pass. And it all becomes perfectly clear to me.

I have no right to be here!

The Rulebook goes bananas and the voice in my head is screaming at me to go back home. Gee has gone to speak to some people so the 'tools' for Taming Tigers are nowhere to be found and the idea that there is anything more scary to be done today than walking into this changing room (full of what have become my heroes in these short months) is ridiculous.

But there are much scarier things to come.

As I head to the gents, Ryan Moore — twice champion jockey since then — seems to be moving in my direction wearing a towel.

Strange.

I ignore him. But he definitely wants to chat.

"Are you riding Theatre of Life?" he asks.

"Yes."

"Go easy on him, he's my sister's favourite horse and he doesn't need you knocking him about. Just let him do as much as he wants."

"It's okay. I'm not going to use my stick at all in case I fall off."

"Good. Enjoy yourself!" And Ryan leaves.

As I get out into the changing room again, Frankie and the others are coming back. I don't think he has been doing a flying dismount. He doesn't look as happy as he does on the TV. I decide against asking for an autograph and start looking for nothing in particular in my bag.

"Jockeys please."

Time to go out. The wind catches you as soon as you leave the weighing room, especially by the seaside. Everybody else is in a coat but we are in silk. Gee has not mentioned the wind. Perhaps it is different for girls.

I meet Gary Moore for the first time. He is a gentleman and puts me at ease. The bell rings and Gary legs me up. Gary Moore, one of the best trainers in the UK has just legged me up onto a racehorse at Brighton Races and I am being led out onto the racetrack by one of his team. I am tempted to shout for joy but then I remember the cheese-grater. Theatre of Life is already jig-jogging along and I have to get this racehorse steadily all the way to the start — a canter of one and a half miles — and then stop him. Or it's Roedean for me. And, perhaps, for the horse. And Ryan won't like that at all. Not at all.

As we go down the chute (the little narrow path between the parade ring and the racecourse) there is a commotion behind us and our groom lets out a little scream. This is unusual around racehorses. I follow her eyes behind me in time to see a rearing, riderless horse (the jockey is flying, colourfully, backwards towards the crowd) break free of the groom leading it up and start to bolt down the chute.

Theatre of Life, my groom and I are creating a cork in a narrow bottleneck. We try to get Theatre of Life to move forward but the horse has planted itself as if it is curious to see what will happen next.

What happens next is that both beasts and me go upwards and then downwards. I remember a sensation like being in a washing machine, hitting the ground and then curling up into a tight ball and wondering if stuff like this ever happened to Frankie. I uncurled slightly to take a look at what was going on around me and saw an eight-legged beast with shiny, sharp metal shoes on flailing about beside me.

I went back to the ball option.

Horses can be quite dainty movers, especially thorough-breds, but they are not at their daintiest when they are trying to get up off of the ground. And especially not when doing it fully tacked up, in a panic and with another horse beside them. I was aware of a few thuds on my body and a few cracks and I somehow found myself looking into the eyes of a beautiful person.

"What's your name?" she asked me.

"Jim," I replied, "What's yours?"

"Don't be cheeky," came the reply. And as I began to focus more clearly, the big green letters on her armband began to form into the word "DOCTOR".

She held up fingers for me to count and then she asked me to follow her index finger as she moved it in front of my face. Finally, she asked my name again to see if I would give the same answer as before. Stupidly, I did. Big mistake.

"Well, Jim, I pronounce you fit to ride."

Now you have to realise that during this process, so happy was I to be able to stand unaided, so delighted was I that I could wiggle my toes, that I had not thought about riding in a horserace. The only thing I had thought about was getting changed and going home. Surely I got to go and have a biscuit now? Just one little drink, perhaps?

"It's good news," she said, "You're fit to ride!"

Clearly this new relationship was not going to work. She had a very different idea of 'good news' to mine. I didn't reckon I could take her 'bad news'!

At the critical moment, Gee appeared over the horizon, jogging over to us. She had been in front of the grandstand and had become curious when I had not cantered past. Gary appeared beside her. Clearly seeing that hesitation to follow Rule 1 and 'act boldly' could lead to her man bailing on her, she grabbed my left ankle and chucked me onto the horse's back. Gary took the leading rein and we were out on the track before you could say, "Cheesegrater".

As I took Theatre of Life down to post, another horse came up on our outer. The rider was in trouble. The horse was bolting and he was swinging off of the back of the thing. Theatre of Life and I had been going a nice steady canter until that point but that set my boy alight and off he went. I eased my weight back and began to pull on the reins, hoping that he would come back to me but as I did so, the reins slipped through the fingers of my right hand. Weird. I looked down. The fact that I had to look at my hand to understand how it was operating should have been a warning sign! But one thing was getting better. I held the horse and watched the other fella bowl off in the direction of Roedean School for Girls.

Well, to cut the story short, your Tiger tamer had pushed the Rulebook a little too far and after his first race he was not going home in glory. Theatre of Life was very slow to start (who could blame him) and we came home 'tailed off' at the back. And after the presentations I was off to hospital, having never been so terrified in all of my life.

Now you may remember that nothing has been said in this book about bravery. That's because I do not feel that I am remotely qualified to write about the subject. And this night proved it. I had never before been as scared as I was when that horse bolted towards us, or when the 'washing machine' feeling began and the two horses and I headed for the deck. And I had certainly never been as scared as was lying on the floor between the horses.

But I was to get more scared a few minutes later when the Roedean end cheesegrater came into sight and I was at full pelt on Theatre of Life with the reins slipping through a clearly broken set of fingers.

I sat there in the hospital wondering if I should continue. I had been on the diet for six months. I had lost nearly a quarter of my bodyweight. I had run almost every day. And I was not only able to run now but I was running up to four miles a day. I could even run convincingly up hills. I had moved house and pitched up in Lambourn telling everybody that I was "going to be a jockey in a year" and not everybody had reacted well to my clumsy cockiness. And now I wanted to quit — more than anything.

I had not bargained on this. I had not expected to break things and go to hospital. I had fallen off a lot at home already and had had some cracking bruises to display but I had not expected to be lying on the floor, in public, with two horses flailing their hooves around my head wearing some silk and paper thin boots for protection. And it was a reality check. I was calculating which way to go, whom I would be letting down, who would mock me if I stopped. I was looking for a way to justify bailing on everybody and on myself.

The phone rang. It was Richard Dunwoody.

I had met Richard in Lambourn and then as a fellow conference speaker. We had become friends and he had also ridden upsides me on the gallops to give me some coaching. For those of you who have no interest in racing, Richard won a couple of Grand Nationals, a Champion Hurdle, a Cheltenham Gold Cup (jump racing's biggest prize) and had been Champion Jockey on three occasions. He also partnered Desert Orchid, perhaps the most famous and best loved horse in European racing to some of his greatest victories.

I saw an opportunity. So, after a few minutes of banter, I asked Richard a question designed to give me some energy.

"So, listen mate."

"Hmm?"

"Why do you think it was you?"

"What?"

"Why was it that you were the champ against all the others riding? What was special about you?"

There was a silence. A long silence. Maybe thirty seconds. I thought that maybe I'd been too personal. But, no, he was having a good think. I don't think he had been asked the question before.

"Well. I think it was me because I wanted it more than anybody else who was riding at the time."

"What?"

"Yep."

"No, come on. Tell me that you worked harder, that you had natural talent, that you were lucky and found great supporters, but don't tell me you just wanted it more."

"Listen mate, I waited five months after my first ride before anybody would let me loose on the racecourse again on one of their horses, so it certainly wasn't natural talent. Sure I had great supporters, but I worked to get and to keep them. And as for luck, I don't think that it's a factor. I wanted that result and I put myself through the mill to get it."

We chatted a little more and I made an excuse to hang up. I needed to think.

Being around Richard, I have learned, is inspiring. He thinks differently. He's unique. He helped me that night more than he will ever know. It was simple! It was not about who I would offend or who would laugh or anything else. It was very simple: did I want to ride in a race on a racetrack under Jockey Club Rules, live on the TV and prove my Rules in the process or not?

If I did, then I should get well and get on a horse as soon as I was able. If I did not, then I should move back to London and stop it all. I did, so the path was clear, the worrying could stop, I could get on with tomorrow.

And that is how Rule 10 was added to the Rules for Taming Tigers:

Never, never give up.

Or give up, but give up on a good day. Give up when the sun is shining and those you value and admire are applauding you for your achievements. And on that day you can turn to them and say, "Thank you. I am now off to train as a nurse. I want to give something back." And off you'll go.

But most of us don't give up on a sunny day. Most of us give up on a stormy day. We give up when the clouds are black and our friends are doubting us and we have to get up at 5am and the rain is horizontal and our partner lies beside us asleep in the bed and she's looking beautiful, and there are doughnuts downstairs. And they look good!

And even if we make it past there we might be forgiven for thinking about giving up when the horse runs away with us and then jinks, dumping us in the mud.

But if we give up on that day, if we take the easier, inviting path, if we take all of the pressure off (as is our right) then we must go to that nursing home by the sea to play cards not knowing.

Not knowing!

Not knowing whether it would have been a year, a month or just a week before we cracked it, before it all came good. We walked off of the track, we gave in, we joined the throng of 'safety in numbers' and sat in the grandstand, telling everybody our view of the other fellas but never getting involved in the action.

The question to you is this: Who is writing your story? You? Me? Or the Tiger that we have created? The Tigers that we build to keep us safe you and I.

What will the difference to your life be if you start to Tame that Tiger today?

Now of course, giving up is a tricky one. The old saying that "there's no use flogging a dead horse" has some sense behind it (inappropriate as it may be in this context) but, the

thing is, in real life we rarely know when the 'horse' is actually dead.

So I'll certainly not be handing out any advice on when
you should decide that enough is enough and that you
should give up on any particular project. What I will pass on
is what I learned on my trip and what others have told me
from their journey.

Giving up has consequences

However you may feel about the chances of picking up your
great project at a later stage, the chances are that you won't.
The chances are that circumstances will have changed, that
friends and supporters will be in a different place, that you
will not be as well prepared — physically and mentally — to
complete the task at any point in the rest of your life as you
are right now.

So the consequence of giving up is very often that you have
reached the end of the affair.

I'll caveat that by saying that I don't know your particular
story, of course, so it may be very different from the way that
you are looking at the world at present.

There are certain times when we should definitely not be giving up

In any attempt to tame your Tigers there will be, by definition, times when the Tiger gets a grip. There will be bad days.
There will be days when you feel as though you have lost all
of your supporters. There will be those days when it is raining
horizontally outside, your lover is curled up alluringly underneath the bedclothes, those doughnuts are in the kitchen and
you're still bruised from the fall you took yesterday.

These are the times when the Tiger picks up the scent of potential defeat and can chase us off of the track. The times when you and I both will be tempted to settle for mediocrity rather than the story we have set our hearts upon. So whilst I shan't be arrogant enough to suggest when you should be calling it a day, I will point out that if you give up when you're feeling the emotion or fatigue that comes from a run of bad days or a run of bad luck, you are giving up in the wrong circumstances.

It may be that it *is* time to give up, but don't take the decision on a bad day. Buy some time, make some excuses, sit by the beach, walk in the park, review these Rules, very, very carefully. Do you need to take a bold action to create some energy (Rule 1)? Are other people's Rulebooks causing you pain, conflict and doubt (Rule 2)? Are you biting off more than you can chew just at the moment? Is the plan clear or in need of tightening to give you certainty? Do you need to give yourself a break and take smaller steps (Rule 3)?

Are the voices running wild in your head? Are they persuading you to do things under pressure that you're going to have to regret for years to come (Rule 4)? Are there people around you that you could be going to for support? And could those people give you practical, tangible support in your project that the Tiger is scaring you away from (Rule 5)? Are you being scared into running with the crowd? You know that there is no safety in numbers and yet is it becoming a little too exposing to be out there (Rule 6)?

How long will it be before the crowd start to move in your direction, to follow you, if you stay on the path that you're on? Are you doing something scary every day? Are you examining, measuring, recalibrating, stretching and flexing your risk muscles? Are you understanding how your brain and body reacts when you're put into a risky situation (Rule 7)? Have you thought through what, in real life, is at stake for you? What is the worst that could happen?

Here are some other signs that giving up at this point may not be the right thing to do:

- You still have a big gut feeling that you are onto something and that there is just a chance that you could pull it off;
- You have allies, people whose opinion you trust and they are urging you to continue;
- You've taken advice, you've received feedback — again, from people whom you trust — and they rate your chances of success at odds that are acceptable to you;
- Rather than losing faith in the project itself, you are being lured by something specific — a particular patch of grass that is looking greener at this moment in time — and you are using this specific and apparently greener grass to give yourself permission to take the pressure off of yourself, to forget about delivering on the thing that you committed to deliver.

Have you thought about the consequences of giving up? Have you carefully thought through what you will be investing your time in if you're not investing it in getting this particular return? What's the return you'll be settling for instead (Rule 8)? Is it acceptable? Is the grass actually greener spending your time doing the other thing?

When the heat is on, it may be time to rely upon your old friend, the basics. Have you identified your disciplines? Are you practising them every day? Can you rely upon those by instinct when you are on the long run in after the last fence, head to head with someone else, and they are all that you have got to rely upon (Rule 9)?

Which brings us back to Rule 10, 'Never, never give up'! Or, at least, never give up until you've stared the consequences long and hard in the face, visited that nursing home by the sea and imagined yourself looking in the mirror and either congratulating yourself for having the wisdom and foresight to have stopped pursuing an impossible dream (that's if you're sure it was impossible) or whether you're wishing you could turn the clock back and take this decision all over again.

The story of your life

You are writing the story of your life. You are the only one holding the pen. You are the sum of your choices to date. You are responsible for your choices today. You are the one making those choices and you have to live with the consequences of those choices and of your actions or inactions tomorrow.

We all have a great story in us.

The primary difference between those who will look back and enjoy having written a great story and those who will look back in disappointment and regret will be whether or not they tamed the Tiger.

I wish you every success and I hope you will wish me the same.

Over to you.

Case study: Catherine McDerment

I work as a Lead Paediatric Occupational Therapist for the NHS in Scotland. The first time I saw Jim speak was two years ago at the end of a six month NHS Education Scotland (NES) Clinical Systems Improvement programme for health professionals. The focus of the course was on improving clinical services delivery using a range of improvement principles and tools, and we all had improvement projects to go away and implement. The focus of my project was improving waiting times for paediatric occupational therapy. Jim was the final speaker on the last day of the course and he was there to motivate us to go off and put our new learning into action, to make us feel that anything is achievable.

> *"In a large organisation like the NHS, there are constant demands and pressures, but it's good to find ways to reach above that. We have added the Ten Rules for Taming Tigers to our team rules as a way of maintaining a positive approach to work."*

When I went along to Jim's talk, I had no preconceptions about motivational speakers, but hadn't experienced anything like it before and wasn't sure what to expect. Jim certainly didn't disappoint! I went away feeling inspired and have continued to feel inspired by his messages, especially his positivity and determination to succeed.

After the talk I emailed Jim to thank him and he sent me some copies of his Taming Tigers cards with the Rules which I shared with my team, who had been inspired by my enthusiasm and feedback from the talk. Sometimes the challenge in a big organisation like the NHS is to maintain peoples' enthusiasm and energy for change and to juggle the many challenges and demands.

Hearing Jim speak renewed my energy and determination to make a difference and to continually strive for improvement in the service we deliver. He helped to remind me that anything is achievable if you learn to look at it in a different way and if you can 'Tame the Tigers' within.

I've used Jim's rules to help with my own personal motivation at work, to look at my personal Rulebook and challenge myself. Since his talk I have been busy rewriting my own Rulebook and challenging everything. If we don't, nothing will ever change. The voices in my head are still there but this time they are reminding me that I can do it and I can do it well.

I have always considered myself to be a positive thinker and I like the positivity of Jim's Rules. In a large organisation like the NHS, there are constant demands and pressures, but it's good to find ways to reach above that. I felt Jim's Rules renewed my positivity and enabled me to share it with my team. In fact, we have since added the Ten Rules for Taming Tigers to our team rules as a way of maintaining a positive approach to work.

My job involves the leadership of a large team of staff as well as a clinical role and I've been able to apply the Rules in all aspects of my work. The Rules I particularly like are Rule 1 (Act boldly today — time is limited), Rule 3 (Head in the direction of where you want to arrive, every day), Rule 7 (Do something scary everyday) and finally Rule 10 (Never, never give up). Rewriting my Rulebook has also been important to me. It's about not being complacent about what you do and challenging it. Equipping yourself with the right tools and speaking to the right people who can influence change is also useful.

Doing something scary every day might not seem appropriate in the NHS. However, I always think, "if you do what you've always done, you get what you've always had" and sometimes you need to radically change what you're doing to make things better. I think everyone will agree there is always scope for improvement. The idea of doing something scary and giving it a go has been really positive. Also, the idea of never ever giving up. Sometimes in a big organisation you can feel that you're not getting anywhere and keeping going is important.

Everyone has days when they wake up and think, "I can't do this" but Jim has planted a little voice in my head as a reminder to challenge it and have the belief and the confidence that I can do it. In the NHS, there are a lot of challenges with resources and demands that we can't always meet and maintaining that confidence and belief are key.

The NHS can be a very positive organisation to work for but it has its challenges and can be quite pressured. You can blame things on resources, but it's not so much resources as resourcefulness that counts in my opinion. You need to have a positive approach to make it work.

When my team get bogged down, the Rules inspire and help us not to give up, which is why we've added them into our staff rules. The rest of my team haven't seen Jim speak but I hope I manage to pass the energy on to them. I also act as a mentor for other teams and have mentioned the Rules to them too.

The NHS is constantly changing, which it needs to do and the Rules can help to support that change and keep the energy flowing. I feel we all need to be empowered to make the NHS the best it can be for everyone. The difference I've noticed in me is a renewed energy about what I'm doing. We all need inspiration and the Ten Rules are inspiration you can use regularly.

Afterword

My first race

On 21st November 2004, the night before my first race, I felt like a condemned man. In fact, probably a little worse than a condemned man — at least he gets a last meal, and I wasn't going to be having much of a dinner.

I packed my bag for the morning, and got a childish satisfaction from, for the first time ever, putting a bag containing saddle, stick, silk breeches, body-protector, skullcap, shiny new permit to ride under Rules, medical book and so on by the door for the morning. A jockey's kit bag.

I went to bed nervous but I woke up with my heart in my throat. The race was at 12pm at Southwell, approximately a four hour drive. I had arranged to pick Gee up at 6am so that we'd have time to walk the track. On the journey, we made the mistake of picking up the Racing Post to see if they were writing about me. They were, and it was a very kind and encouraging piece, but it was the wrong time to read it. The pressure was mounting.

We arrived at Southwell Racecourse and parked in the jockey's car park area (another first) and I get my bag from the boot and stride with Gee towards the Weighing Room. All the track staff, stable staff, trainers and jockeys seem to know Gee and they are nodding at her and waving. It's like walking through Leicester Square with Madonna! We get to the Weighing Room and I sign in. Walking into the Weighing Room is something I never got used to; just a huge buzz and a huge privilege to get changed next to these people. I say "hi" to Marmite who is my valet today and whom I had met at Brighton. Totally unexpectedly, he seems to tune in to the fact that I'm on edge and is immediately warm and reassuring. There's an hour to go. I meet Gee outside and we walk the track together.

As we walk around the fibresand surface (you can't really check where the ground is best on the all weather track, so there's not that much to look at as we wander round — I'm just getting my bearings), Gee calms me down brilliantly. She exudes confidence in me. I don't know why she does — but I am very glad and grateful. It helps. We go through, once again, the key things to remember. Grab hold of the mane as the stalls open. Leave him a nice long length of rein so you don't jab his mouth. Have you agreed the race tactics with Charlie? Don't stop riding until you pass the finishing line whatever you do. Don't be put off by the Tannoy when you come into the home-straight. Don't be tempted to use your stick — don't even pick it up on your first race, I've seen people fall off. Hands and heels all the way. And then we're past the finishing line and I'm heading back to the Weighing Room.

I get changed and sit on the wooden bench under my peg. I thought I had time on my side, but everything's happening more quickly now. Marmite wants me to do a trial weigh-out, to check how much lead I'm going to have to carry. Charlie's arrived with the silks and Marmite's put the white silk on my hat and draped the jacket over my peg while we've been walking. I get changed to do the trial weigh-out, and Marmite asks if I want any elastic bands.

"What for?" I ask.

He laughs, "because your silk is too long for your arms You don't want it falling down over your hands!"

"Okay. Elastic bands, please."

I weigh out, and I've never been so pleased to see Charlie's face; he's standing in the Weighing Room by the scales. He gives a broad grin and a wink as he picks up the saddle and weight-cloth and heads off to saddle up Airgusta.

Back to the wooden bench in the Weighing Room. Nerves have kicked in quite hard now. A lot of people that I don't want to let down have helped, have poured their heart and soul into making this day arrive. I think through the phases of the job. First, the parade-ring, then the chute, getting down to post, keeping him calm at the start, loading up and jumping out of the stalls. And then there are the different personalities of the race itself: jockeying for position, sticking pretty much tight in that position as the race unfolds and then, finally, either dictating or reacting as you begin to come close to home. And then hell for leather for the finish.

I'm sitting on the bench, lost in these thoughts when I hear my name called out. I don't recognise the man in the suit who's calling my name, and he's looking blindly around the Weighing Room without a clue who I am. I put my hand up and say, "yes," and suddenly realise that I look like a schoolboy. He asks if he can have a word and we go outside to the

Clerk of the Scales' table together. Now I do feel like a schoolboy following the headmaster outside and it is not easing my nerves.

"I'm the Starter," he introduces himself, "and I want to speak to you about the procedure down at the start to make sure you understand it."

Now we've been through this at the British Racing School, and Gee and I have gone through it together a hundred times at home, but I'm surprised at how happy I am to hear him say this. He talks me through everything from arriving at the stalls, loading, and then he begins to describe what he'll do to start the race.

"So I'll call, 'Jockeys!' and then, if there are any blindfolds, I'll call 'Blindfolds!', and then you'll see my flag drop and the stall-gates will open. Is that clear?"

"Clear, thanks. Except . . . hold on! What if there are no blindfolds? What will you shout then?"

"Then I'll just shout, 'Jockeys!' and the next thing will be that the stall-gates will open."

He's making me nervous. In one situation he'll shout the equivalent of "Ready, Steady, Go" but, if there are no blindfolds, it's going to be the equivalent of "Ready — Go." And I'm still going to be waiting for "Steady!" Brilliantly, he's got my problem and understands it entirely without me saying anything more.

"Okay, Jim. Whatever happens today, I will shout, 'Jockeys! Blindfolds!' And then it's the flag. Happy?"

I resist the urge to give him a hug and, instead, reply, "Happy."

And I'm back on the wooden bench waiting.

"Jockeys for the first, jockeys for the first!"

I feel my stomach lurch, get up and walk out of the Weighing Room. To my amazement I'm getting some good luck shouts from the other lads, and a massive smile and a raised clenched fist from Marmite.

I hadn't been prepared for how cold it would be in November wearing nothing but silk, or how totally naked you feel as the wind seems to whip around your skin. I'm just adjusting to this as I see Charlie and Gee standing in the middle of the parade-ring. They have great big grins on their faces as I wander over and it is so good to see them. Caroline is leading Airgusta round the outside and he looks a picture. Charlie asks me if I can remember the tactics. We're running Airgusta, a two-miler, over a mile simply because the team want to help me win my bet. This race is a year to the day since I met Gee at the Swan in Great Shefford and it all started. I repeat the plan back to Charlie.

"Yes. Use him up as fast as I like, get to the front as quick as I can, stay there and kick out all the way home, because he doesn't have any turn of foot (no acceleration). He only has one pace, so we need to use it all the way."

"Spot on." Charlie reassures me.

The bell rings. Gee, rather than Charlie, legs me up — she's my lucky mascot today — and Caroline leads us out onto the track.

Airgusta's on his toes and moving sideways down the chute, but this is nothing that he hasn't done walking onto the gallops at home, so I'm not too worried. In fact, I'm amazed at how much happier I am sitting up here in the saddle than I was in the parade-ring. Perhaps it's down to that Rule 4 trick, 'get lost in the task rather than analysing it' — that we spoke about all those chapters ago. I was, now I look back, totally absorbed in the task. We canter past the grand-stand, pull up, turn around and canter round to the one mile start.

We load up. Airgusta is first in, and he loads like an angel. The gates shut behind us and he stands alert but still, wait-ing. And I am waiting also. And the strangest thing to me, as I sit in the stalls waiting, is the view that I have. I've sat in the stalls often enough at school in Newmarket and at home in Lambourn, but I have never sat in them on a racetrack before, and I find myself totally unprepared for the different view. In front of me now, instead of a grassy field with some trees at the other end that I'd better pull up in good time to avoid hitting, I have the back-straight at Southwell Racecourse. It is the first race of the day, so the track is freshly harrowed and looks like a beach after the tide has gone out and the sun has dried it off. Granted, it's not Goodwood, but to me at this moment it's an amazing view and, perhaps for the first time, the race itself becomes very real.

In a few seconds, we'll get to make the first hoof prints of the day on the deep fibresand and, if the plan goes right, I'll be tight against the rails at the front. In a horserace. What'll it be like?

We've drawn Stall One, which gives our plan a better chance of success. It's very unlikely that this good natured stayer that I'm sitting on would be able to beat the milers that he is lined up against. The bookies have us at 50–1 for that very reason (perhaps not helped by a new rider on his back), but if I can jump off smartly enough and get him up to a pace that no miler will want to be at just yet, we've cer-tainly a chance of landing mid-division or better.

One of the lads calls out, "Who's making the running?"

"I am." I call back.

I turn my head around and there are three left to load and they are all being led forward. Maybe five seconds unless one refuses. I can feel my heart beating against my body-protector, but everybody else looks as though they're having a day at the office. I've never been in the stalls with more than one other horse, and as they load, the whole structure begins to move as different animals behave in different ways in their stall. My legs are tight up against the side, so every time a horse makes the structure move, my leg gets crushed against the wall. It's not that it hurts, it's just that it's weird and not what I'm expecting — I'm miles outside of my safety zone. I'm amazed to find that all I want to do now is get out of the stalls and get on with the race.

"Two to load! One to load! Loaded!"

Breathe. Long rein. Grab the mane. Take the weight into my feet but don't leave saddle.

"Jockeys! Blindfolds!"

I can sense some of the guys looking round a bit puzzled — there's not a blindfold in sight. Then there it is. That familiar snap of the gates. Familiar from all those trips down to the start, familiar from Newmarket and from Lambourn.

And there it is. That burst of speed, but it's faster, much faster than anything he's done at home. And I'm riding him already, scrubbing along and shouting in his ear to get him up to speed, just as I've done so many times on the equicizer with Jason Cook in the gym in Lambourn, simulating getting the horse into his stride in the early part of the race. Gee has had us working on this ever since we knew it was going to be a mile race on a two-miler.

We reach the first bend tight against the rails with a lead of a length and a half, cruising nicely, and for a moment I stop to enjoy it. For a moment it's very simple, very peaceful and, for a deluded moment, I even get the feeling that I know what I'm doing here. Out in front at Southwell, all I can hear is the sound of Airgusta's hooves and the sound of wind. I can't hear any other horses behind me, just the wind. It's like hurtling downhill on a bicycle with a skull cap on that doesn't cover your ears and, again, it's a noise that I've never experienced before. Even that first rush of wind that I felt as Victor ran off with me at Jamie Osborne's, and which seemed so loud at the time, turns out to have been a gust compared to the tornado that's going past my ears now. I even have time to notice how deep the track is at Southwell. The hollow of Airgusta's hoof is making a thud into the sand as it hits the ground.

But the thudding is now getting decidedly louder. We're on the long, sweeping turn, and in a matter of seconds we're going to be on the home-straight. It is a complete delusion, after all, I've been distracted, perhaps for less than two seconds, by all of the new sensations, and that's not allowed in a horserace. And I'm about to get punished for it. First there's one, then there's two, suddenly three horses are upsides me. We're almost touching. Down in the saddle, change hands, Airgusta picks up the bit and does his best to go with them, but we're on the milers' home territory now, and I should have been working him far harder from far earlier round that long, sweeping bend. The horses with two gears are using them to our disadvantage.

He's working really hard (I thought I was too, until I saw the video after the race, and was very disappointed at how weak I looked in that first race), but one's got past us, now two. For the first time in the race he's got kick-back — his muzzle, his eyes and my face are beginning to be covered in sand. I look down to take a quick gasp of clean air before coming head-on again, this time to be met by the noise of the Tannoy; another unexpected sound. Two horses upsides us now, three in front, the Tannoy beginning to be much louder than the hooves. Five in front now, fourteen in the race, perhaps I can hold sixth? Another new sound is all around me, the sound of sticks being used.

Then another strange sound, the roar of the crowd. Nothing prepares you for this, even at Southwell. I cannot imagine what it must be like to ride into this sound as you come up the home straight at Ascot.

The two red lollipops are getting closer and I need them now. To be honest, Airgusta could probably do this for a little while longer. He's only just getting into his stride and I probably haven't made as much use of him early on as I could have done, but my thighs, despite all the work on the equicizer, are on fire.

"Don't stop riding until you've past the line". And I don't.

And it's done. I'm trying to pull him up. I stand up in my irons and ease my weight back and I'm amazed to find that my legs are working just fine. I've seen newcomers buckle as they try to stand up and it's not something I wanted to do. Thanks Gee and thanks Jason.

And then it strikes me. We've done it.

We've bloody done it!

And I'm not the only one who's realising this. As we turn and canter back to the chute, ease into a trot, and finally come to a walk, Gee and Caroline are jumping up and down and beaming where the chute meets the track. And seeing their reaction sets me off too. Absolute elation! None of us can quite believe that we have finally made it. Gee beams up at me and reaches her hand up. I don't have the confidence to put my right hand over the left side of the horse, so I shake hands with my left hand and try to speak.

Then I realise that I can't. It's not that I'm welling up here, it's that my mouth has simply never been this dry — the mixture of nerves and sand means that I am completely unable to speak. It's welded shut.

The journey back to unsaddle and eventually the walk to the Weighing Room is quite surreal. Strangers are waving at me and saying "well done". I guess they've seen the paper or heard the commentary and have been wishing me well. As I walk back past the 'At The Races' commentary team's position for the day, Simon Mapletoft and Jason Weaver ask if I'll come straight back out when I've dumped my kit and talk to the cameras. Now that I hadn't expected at all, and given the fact that I'm not actually able to speak at this moment sets me back into another stomach clamp of nerves.

In the Weighing Room, there are lots of congratulations for me and I'm really touched by everyone's reaction. Racing really is an extraordinary place. I dump my stuff on my peg and turn round to find Marmite giving me a big, broad grin and telling me he wants those elastic bands back.

I get a plastic cup of water from the jug on the table, swill it round my mouth to get rid of the sand and see if I can get my tongue to come back to life before going out to talk to the TV presenters.

And as I do so, in the first real quiet moment since the race ended, it dawns on me at last that calling up a raft of strangers and asking for help, moving house, losing a quarter of my bodyweight, getting as fit as a flea, learning to ride, breaking bones at Brighton Racecourse and getting up at 5am every day has all been completely worthwhile.

We won the bet. We did it!

We formed an amazing team, Gee, Bos, Sarah Bosley, Charlie Morlock, Tina Fletcher, Jason Cook, Michael, many others and I. And we formed friendships that have endured. And we did it.

And also, along the way, the Ten Rules for Taming Tigers were proven.

About the Author

Jim Lawless is one of Europe's most popular inspirational speakers and the only speaker to have put his money where his mouth is to prove his theories. In response to an audience challenge he went from overweight non-riding consultant to his first televised horserace under Jockey Club Rules in twelve months to prove that Taming Tigers worked.

Jim began his career as a corporate lawyer in the City of London but after seven years of jokes about his surname he founded the change consultancy Optimise (now Taming Tigers Group) of which he is CEO. He has worked with individuals and groups within organisations including Apple, Barclays, Siemens, IBM, the NHS, Rolls Royce, RBS, Unilever, Deloitte, Marks and Spencer, Experian, Linklaters, Procter and Gamble and Sun Microsystems. In 2008 he launched the innovative Taming Tigers Learning training methodology.

He rides regularly, plays the piano and guitar badly, really enjoys eating previously banned things and avoids taking bets from audience members.

About Sparks and Racing Welfare

Sparks

Sparks is the children's medical research charity. Their sole remit is to fund research across the whole spectrum of paediatric medicine. Their goal is for all babies to be born healthy and stay healthy.

They raise money to give all babies the best start in life — a healthy one. Their research, which is carried out by leading doctors and researchers nationwide, is saving and improving the lives of children throughout the world.

Their vision is for a world where all babies are given the best possible start in life and where a medical condition or disability at birth is not a barrier to opportunity and fulfilment. They achieve this by funding high quality medical research that is intended to have a practical and positive effect on the lives of children.

To learn more about Sparks please go to www.sparks.org.uk.

Racing Welfare.

Racing Welfare is recognised as Racing's leading welfare charity providing an accessible, responsive and professional occupational welfare service to all of Racing's people including employers, employees and the retired.

They support all the unsung heroes who form the backbone of the racing industry. These include not just stud and stable staff, but also gallop men and racecourse staff.

Racing Welfare deliver accessible, responsive and professional counselling, advice and financial assistance for those who suffer illness, injury or other disadvantage. They promote healthy living and wellbeing and have developed access to affordable housing.

To learn more about Racing Welfare please go to www.racingwelfare.co.uk or call 01638 560763.

More praise for Taming Tigers

"inspirational and human all at once"
Miriam Byrne
Director, City Analysts Ltd

"engaging, challenging, inspiring . . . a practical, compelling model for achieving results"
Gary Hoffman
Group Vice Chairman, Barclays Bank

"a masterclass in taking control and accepting personal responsibility in the management of change"
Paul Snell
Chief Inspector, Commission for Social Care Inspection

"dynamic and engaging"
Jayne Stokes
Head Of Learning & Development, Alliance & Leicester Commercial Bank

"Everybody should know the Ten Rules for Taming Tigers. Extraordinary."
Gee Armytage
Champion Lady Jockey, Racing Legend

"challenging and inspiring"
Ian Dyson
Finance Director, Marks and Spencer plc

"animated, motivating and funny"
H. S. H. Prince Max von und zu Liechtenstein, LGT Group CEO

"inspiring and refreshingly different"
David Birrell
Marketing Manager, J&J Haslett Ltd

"thought provoking, empowering and entertaining"
Mike Green
Deputy Group Finance Director, ITV PLC